Praise for *Navigate Your Career*

"With *Navigate Your Career*, Dr. Shveta Miglani has crafted a comprehensive roadmap to success. Her deep understanding of career development and her inspirational guidance make this book a must-read."

—Siva Sivaram,
President and CEO of Quantum Space

"Whether you are well established in your career or just getting started, Dr. Shveta Miglani's *Navigate Your Career* serves as an indispensable guide for thriving in a new role. Through deeply researched insights and relatable personal stories from those who have been through it, Miglani masterfully unpacks the hard truths of navigating career transitions, offering readers practical advice and recipes for success."

—Drew Henry,
Executive Vice President Strategy and Ecosystems at ARM

"Dr. Miglani's comprehensive and structured approach is a must-read for anyone pursuing a successful career or role change. Her insights are invaluable for charting a progressive career path."

—Shiva Esturi,
Vice President at Micron Technology

"With *Navigate Your Career*, Dr. Shveta Miglani shares 7 practical strategies to take charge of your success. Her insightful stories give every reader a clear way to evaluate, define, and achieve success at every step of their career."

—Humera Malik Shahid,
Vice President Talent Development and,
Inclusion – Western digital

"This book is a must-read for anyone stepping into a new role. Dr. Shveta Miglani masterfully combines compelling storytelling with practical advice, delivering career lessons that will empower you to hit the ground running and achieve success."

—Lorraine K. Lee,
Keynote Speaker and author of *Unforgettable Presence*

"Shveta Miglani is the real deal. Shveta has spent 20 years in and around HR in one of the roughest, toughest environments for "People": high tech in Silicon Valley. She's seen dozens of high potentials succeed. . . and fail. Many smart people simply do their jobs and let their career manage them. Listen and learn from one of the rock stars in high-tech talent management. She can help YOU manage and OWN your career!"

—Jack B. Keenan,
Founder and Chairman of Jack B. Keenan Inc.

"In *Navigate Your Career*, Dr. Shveta Miglani makes an incisive connection between how we move from our philosophical understanding of success to a strategic implementation of success. This playbook delivers a vertical and horizontal approach to making an impact in your career, adapting to environments and cultures, and finding your pathways to success by defining clear goals and being willing to do the work necessary to get there."

—Sharawn Tipton,
Chief People and Culture Officer, LiveRamp

"Shveta Miglani's *Navigate Your Career* feels like having a personal coach in your corner. It's packed with sharp, practical strategies that cut through the noise and set you up to thrive in any new role. If you're stepping into something new and want to crush it from day 1, this is the playbook you need."

—AJ Thomas,
Founder and CEO, The Troublemaker Lab

"Dr. Shveta Miglani has such a wealth of experience in developing and coaching talent in the corporate world and understands both sides of developing a successful career. Her new book, *Navigate Your Career*, is the perfect guide for anyone starting a new job or career or who is looking to jump-start their career to accelerate their success. I highly recommend it."

—Andy Storch,
author of *Own Your Career Own Your Life*

"I thoroughly enjoyed reading Dr. Miglani's book, and several sections really resonated with me. One example is her insight into the important questions we should ask both our boss and ourselves when starting a new job. As she wisely states, "Knowing what is expected of you allows you to focus your efforts effectively."

—Ashima Puri,
People Team Operations and Chief
of Staff, Samsung Electronics

"A practical and insightful guide for anyone stepping into a new role. This book offers valuable strategies that can help you start strong and succeed with confidence."

—Marc Effron,
President, Talent Strategy Group,
and author of *One Page Talent Management*

"Shveta's expertise as a leader in Learning and Development shines in this relatable and practical career guide—perfect for professionals at all stages."

—Trena Minudri,
Chief Learning Officer, Coursera

""Navigate Your Career" is a powerful guide for ambitious professional striving for advancement. Shveta Miglani offers actionable strategies and inspiring stories to help you to achieve new roles and earn well-deserved promotions. A must-have for anyone serious about career growth."

—Pavitra Rungta,
Operations and Product Finance — Apple

NAVIGATE YOUR CAREER

NAVIGATE YOUR CAREER

STRATEGIES FOR SUCCESS
IN NEW ROLES AND PROMOTIONS

SHVETA MIGLANI, PhD

WILEY

Published by John Wiley & Sons, Inc., Hoboken, New Jersey.
Published simultaneously in Canada.

Library of Congress Cataloging-in-Publication Data is Available:

ISBN 9781394357864 (Cloth)
ISBN 9781394357871 (ePub)
ISBN 9781394357888 (ePDF)

Cover Design: Wiley
Cover Images: Star map: © tyndyra/Getty Images
  Page rip: © WhataWin/Getty Images

SKY10120356_070725

For Kabeer and Mrinal, my universe

Contents

Contents

If you can dream—and not make dreams your master,
If you can think—and not make thoughts your aim,
If you can meet with Triumph and Disaster and treat those
two impostors just the same. . .

—Excerpt from "If" by Rudyard Kipling

Prologue

A journey of a thousand miles begins with a single step.

—Lao Tzu

AT THE AGE OF 27, I received a job offer from one of the best companies in the world after several months of interviews. I thought this was my dream job. This company was ramping up to be a software giant. I had studied all its products, learned about its culture through available videos, freshened up my educational technical skills, and spent hours practicing in front of the mirror to answer questions. When the job offer arrived, I accepted the role, moved to another city, and left my friends and family behind.

During the interview process, adrenaline surged through me, fueling my excitement. I carried that energy with me as I stepped through the door on my first day of orientation, eager to meet everyone, absorb as much as possible about the business, and prove myself as a valuable addition to the team. The feeling of fitting in was important to me because I thought I would do my job well if I fit in. In my mind, I had made it, and all my hard work was finally showing results. The one thought that kept me going was that my family would be so proud of me for getting a job at one of the best tech companies in the world.

The feeling didn't last long. After my first 100 days, I realized I had made a big mistake and didn't see myself staying there. What went wrong? What could I have done better? Was I not capable of taking on that role? Why didn't I succeed in that company?

These thought-provoking questions have often kept me awake at night as I've reflected on my professional journey. Over the course of several years as a talent development leader, I've had the opportunity to create global leadership development programs and collaborate with seasoned executives and newcomers across various organizations. What struck me the most was that, like me, they were seeking answers to a fundamental question: "What leads to success in a new role?"

With over two decades of experience in talent development, I've observed that someone usually knows within the first two to three months if they are going to stay in an organization. I have devoted my life to understanding the intricacies of joining new companies and assuming fresh roles. Not only have I meticulously planned my own transitions based on personal experience, but I have also designed and implemented onboarding programs across various global organizations to make the new employees successful in their new jobs. These programs allowed me to learn from both seasoned leaders and fellow newcomers, gaining insights into how they prepare for their responsibilities.

Due to my interest in the topic and with the mission of improving outcomes, I observed the journeys of these individuals within their respective companies. To validate my findings, I conducted rigorous doctoral research focused on answering the question I mentioned earlier: "What contributes to success in a new role?" This comprehensive study involved analyzing published data, conducting numerous interviews, and seeking peer evaluation. But I didn't want to merely publish a dissertation. I took the research further and conducted interviews with industry leaders about their experience in order to share the best strategic tools for you to be successful in your next role. The result is this book, so you can benefit from their knowledge.

A Fish in New Waters

When I tell people I have changed residential addresses 22 times in my lifetime, they are shocked. A huge part of those changes in my young years was due to my father's government job in India. With every promotion he received, we landed in a new city. As you can imagine, I had to settle into a new home, a new set of friends, and a new school each time we moved. Even now, when I smell fresh paint, I'm taken back to the moments in my life when I used to walk into a new home filled with moving boxes, and friendly neighbors who would stop by to greet us. These moves helped me learn new languages and learn about the different cultures of the cities where we lived. At a young age, without knowing the technical term for what I was learning, I had started the process of gathering the knowledge to assimilate in a new place. At the same time, I had started to create a mental playbook to help me expedite that process more quickly.

To fit in, I sharpened my elevator pitch, which helped me to make new friends almost every day. While going up and down our apartment elevators, I would meet our new neighbors. In my case, my ability to share an elevator pitch really and truly did start in elevators. This important skill served me well because I had someone's attention for just a few minutes. The skill can serve you well because you want to leave a good impression and you want people to remember you the next time they see you.

Based on each person's reaction in the elevator, I modified my approach to introducing myself. This was real-time learning. For instance, using humor to introduce myself always helped me feel more at ease, breaking the ice and creating a comfortable atmosphere. While this approach landed well with people my age, older people didn't appreciate it. The type of language I used also mattered because, in India, we communicate in several languages. For instance, when I met kids my age, I would introduce myself in

English with a joke or two about how we'd be lucky if the elevator takes us up safely and doesn't stop in the middle. I would always get a chuckle from others my age. By the time we reached our floors, we would have progressed from strangers to acquaintances. However, when I introduced myself to older people in the neighborhood, I greeted them in Hindi with a "Namaste" first. I talked with them about which school I was attending, which the older generation wanted to know. I stayed away from making *any* jokes about elevators because that would not have gone over well with them. Making friends in these new places and networking with them helped me and my family learn about the local issues, such as where we could find the best schools, restaurants, groceries, and social events in the community. This reduced the time needed for us to feel comfortable in our new location. This was the era of no internet, and getting access to information depended on conversations and relationships; it was not as easy as it is now. After my "elevator work," I was able to walk to the bus and say hello to new acquaintances. This increased my confidence to do better and took my mind off of feeling like a newbie.

Building skills around how to communicate with my target audience helped me to assimilate into my new surroundings and gave me the confidence to fit in. When I was younger, this process was fun and felt like an adventure with every new place. As I hit my teen years, the situation became tougher. Rather than starting a new adventure, fitting in became the central focus for every move. Remember, this was the era with no internet (I know I am dating myself here), no social media (obviously), and no way to learn about a new city, the residential area, or my school in advance. I could not prepare for the transition in advance, and I had to jump into the situation with both feet.

In over two decades of working at various organizations within the corporate world, the concept of fitting in has remained a constant.

As I transitioned between roles, this feeling persisted, shaping my professional journey. I began this journey by gaining hands-on experience at some of the top Silicon Valley companies, complementing that real-world learning with academic research to deepen my understanding.

Over the years, I had the privilege of contributing to the success of several Fortune 500 companies. Among them were Salesforce, GlobalFoundries, SanDisk, Palo Alto Networks, LiveRamp, and Micron. My diverse roles centered around optimizing employee performance and driving business revenue. I achieved this by collaborating with cross-functional teams, including business units, sales, marketing, and human resources.

Building skills around how to communicate with my target audience helped me to assimilate into my new surroundings and gave me the confidence to fit in.

Some of these companies offered the best benefits, satisfying roles, and invigorating onboarding sessions. Even though from the outside these organizations had everything to offer, I would know in a matter of weeks if I wasn't going to stay long term with the company. When this happened early in my career, I wasn't able to decipher why I did not like the new job. Reflecting on my experience after several years, I realized that the companies where I didn't want to stay were the ones where I could not fit in for a variety of reasons. My experience turned into scientific curiosity, and this led me to design a study in my postgraduate work about what makes someone successful in their role.

Throughout my professional journey, I've encountered numerous opportunities for advancement that have enriched my expertise. My graduate research and the privilege of guiding various leaders as an executive coach during their transitional phases have been particularly formative. These experiences equipped me with a wealth of knowledge that I am eager to share.

When I think about adjusting to new places and within a new company, I am reminded of a wonderful story that I would like to share. My dad was very fond of exotic fishes and we had a large fish tank in our home, right next to our dining area. Instead of watching TV or reading, my dad loved having his meals and watching his fish enjoying their surroundings in the tank he built. He found this relaxing. Every few months, my sister and I would go to the fish tank store in our city with great excitement to find the next pair of fish to add to our fish tank. This tradition helped us to understand more about these creatures and what it takes to help them thrive.

One day, my mom surprised us all by bringing home a pair of goldfish. We were all excited to see how they would enjoy their new tank. As we were slowly putting them in the tank, my dad had a big smile on his face as he was enjoying the process.

He said, "Now we have to wait and see how the fish acclimatize to the new tank."

My sister and I giggled and teased our dad that "acclimatize" wasn't a word, and he was creative for making it up. "Why don't you girls go look it up in your dictionary?" he asked.

We promptly ran to our room and, of course, we were so excited to see the word and what it meant. According to the dictionary, "acclimatize" means to respond physiologically or behaviorally to a change in conditions in the natural environment. This fun situation helped me to learn a new word and to understand what I was going through when I later changed jobs and joined a new company. Many of you will face the same situation and will want to acclimatize to your new surroundings quickly, so you can thrive and not merely survive. I am also happy to report that the fish quickly settled in, and, within a few days, they were happily swimming around the tank, enjoying the company of their new aquatic friends and their new home.

Starting a new chapter in your career is an adventure. This book acts as your guide through the unknown terrain of a fresh corporate environment and position. I write this to help you gain an understanding of a company's culture, anticipated standards, and the subtle nuances that often take extensive time to discern. The Navigate Your Career approach focuses on creating an optimal beginning to a new position, making sure you distinguish yourself as someone ready to make a significant contribution. The process I teach here transcends merely securing a position and helps you master the position from your first day.

The Navigate Your Career approach focuses on creating an optimal beginning to a new position, making sure you distinguish yourself as someone ready to make a significant contribution.

How to Benefit from This Book

As we grow, we revisit certain books. They serve as mental refreshers, catalysts for new learning, and guides for applying concepts in the evolving context of our lives. My hope is that this book becomes that type of valuable resource for you. Whether you're an intern, an experienced professional, an individual contributor, a knowledge worker, or a leader, the insights within these pages are universally applicable.

Navigating your career involves taking control of your professional path, making thoughtful decisions, and confidently driving actions toward growth and success. This process demands a proactive mindset, a readiness to embrace responsibility, and the ability to inspire and motivate oneself and others. Navigating your career in a new role begins with evaluating the current landscape, understanding potential challenges, and identifying opportunities to make meaningful progress.

This book is intentionally crafted to empower you with the flexibility to engage with the content in a manner that suits your preferences. You can opt to read it sequentially, page by page, or directly dive into specific strategies that resonate with your situation.

Introduction

By failing to prepare, you are preparing to fail.

—Benjamin Franklin

ON MARCH 30, 1994, INDRA NOOYI joined her new role as a corporate strategist at PepsiCo. Before PepsiCo, she had worked for quite a few years as a product manager and strategic consultant at companies like Johnson & Johnson, Motorola, Boston Consulting Group, and ABB. She was an experienced professional when she joined PepsiCo. In the first few months of starting her role, she did all the right things. She met with her team and department heads and, most important, she asked questions of her boss about PepsiCo's finances, structure, and priorities. Doing this helped her to excel in her role and to use all the key resources around her to learn about PepsiCo's culture and its people. She met the team in different locations around the world in her initial months to learn directly from the source about the inner workings of different functions. She put in hours to study, prepare, and continue to learn by surrounding herself with various resources and giving it all she had.

Nooyi knew, to ramp up in her new role, she would need to invest equal time in all the areas, stakeholders, and the business. She went on to become the CEO of PepsiCo from 1996 to 2012, and one could say her initial steps of strategizing in her new role helped to lay that foundation. Nooyi's example serves as a powerful reminder that, regardless of your level in your professional career, strategically planning your path before joining a job is a crucial investment of your time.

Regardless of your level in your professional career, strategically planning your path before joining a job is a crucial investment of your time.

Evolution of Work

Since the late 18th century, the Industrial Revolution has profoundly transformed work, shifting it from agrarian economies to industrialized urban centers. Factories centralized production, introducing mass manufacturing techniques that demanded long hours—often 12 to 16 hours a day, six days a week—with low wages and little regard for worker safety. Child labor was prevalent, and working conditions were hazardous. Despite these grueling hours, wages were meager, with men earning slightly more than women, and children, who also worked in factories, earning the least. The factory environment was hazardous, with little regard for worker safety, as machines lacked safety covers and accidents were common. Children as young as five were employed to operate machinery, often because their small fingers could handle delicate tasks. In Norman Ware's book, The Industrial Worker 1840-1860, he highlights about the working conditions during the Industrial Revolution. Factory workers, including children, endured long hours—sometimes exceeding 12 to 16 hours a day—with minimal breaks. The work environments were poorly ventilated, dimly lit, and filled with hazardous machinery, leading to frequent injuries. Employers prioritized efficiency over worker safety, and labor laws were virtually nonexistent. Over time, labor movements and government regulations improved conditions, but the early years of industrialization were marked by exploitation and hardship.

Over time, these harsh realities spurred the rise of labor unions and movements advocating for workers' rights, better wages, and safer working environments. Today, the work landscape has changed dramatically. Modern workplaces typically feature standard eight-hour workdays, five days a week, with paid holidays and vacation time. Strict safety regulations and labor laws now protect workers, who receive fair wages, health insurance, retirement plans, and other benefits. A greater emphasis on work-life balance has become more common and includes flexible working hours and remote work options.

Today, companies allocate substantial resources to identify and hire the right candidates for their job openings. These resources encompass financial investments, equity, time, and energy. This holds particularly true in high-growth organizations, where the competition for top talent is fierce. Each new hire represents a significant financial commitment for the company even before they officially begin their role. Research consistently shows that the highest turnover rates within organizations occur among newcomers. Even if a company experiences just a few instances of turnover, the associated costs—both in terms of hiring and training—are substantial.

Organizations are keenly aware of the significant resources they invest in hiring and onboarding new employees. They are committed to your success and have put in place various processes, resources, and support systems to help you thrive. However, your active engagement and proactive approach are crucial to fully benefit from this supportive environment. As you embark on your new role, remember that your success is directly tied to the company's ability to achieve its business goals.

Starting a new professional chapter, whether it's a shift within your current organization or a leap to a new one, requires a strategic approach. The foundational elements of this process are largely the same, though each path demands specific considerations.

> *As you embark on your new role, remember that your success is directly tied to the company's ability to achieve its business goals.*

Take Brandon Clark, for example. His insights from his career trajectory have been invaluable. As the head of global learning and development at Adobe, Brandon's prior experiences at Walmart and Workday provided him with unique perspectives on navigating career transitions.

In our conversation for this book, Brandon recounted his strategies for success when moving between roles. At Walmart, he experienced several internal role changes, where the expectation to dive in and perform was intense, leaving little room for reflection. However, his move to Workday marked a significant change, as he took a six-week hiatus to reflect and strategize, crafting a detailed notebook during this period.

During our book interviews, he emphasized the importance of self-promotion but noted that the true test comes with the actual work. Questions like "Why does the company need me?" and "What unique contributions can I bring?" were central to his preparation.

Brandon opened up about the doubts that surface after a long tenure with one company, questioning one's ability to succeed elsewhere. This is a nod to the phenomenon of "imposter syndrome," a term introduced in the late 1970s by psychologists Pauline Rose Clance and Suzanne Imes. The term describes an individual's internal conflict when they doubt their capabilities despite evident success, a common experience during promotions or when taking on larger responsibilities. This feeling is far more common than most people realize, affecting everyone from entry-level employees to seasoned executives. It's that nagging doubt that despite your achievements, you're not as competent as others perceive you to be. Even some of the most successful leaders have faced these same feelings, proving that imposter syndrome is just a part of the human experience.

Through his period of reflection, Brandon was able to align his thoughts and bolster his confidence for his new role at Workday. His commitment to continuous learning didn't halt when he joined the new company. He keenly observed the organizational dynamics, engaged with key stakeholders early, and crafted a vision for his team, all actions that were instrumental in his successful transition. His time at Workday was a big success as he created a strong impact through his work, built a team of leaders, and continued to achieve personal success in his career journey. He took those learnings to his role at Adobe and today he is a successful leader there.

Career Planning

Let's take a moment to pause before diving into the rest of the chapters and discuss the concept of career planning, which is something I knew little about early in my career. Planning helps you find the right role and achieve success. With online tools like LinkedIn, professionals have more opportunities to seek new careers than before. However, without a strategy, these tools can cause confusion and lead to poor decisions. Being approached by recruiters online can feel validating, yet be cautious about making jumps without thoroughly considering what you want in your next career move. Although you might choose to engage with a recruiter who reached out to you, you need to develop a plan to be ready to accept the *right* offer.

As an executive career coach, I often get questions from clients about when to change jobs or which option to choose between two offers. For example, I worked with a finance leader in his early 30s who moved to the United States for a new role with his current company. The company had been supportive, giving him additional projects and opportunities to learn. When he approached me, he had the option to stay in his current role and wait for a promotion his manager had verbally promised or take another role with higher prospects of exposure and learning, which came with a promotion. He was torn and unable to focus as this decision weighed heavily on his mind.

I asked him to list his "must haves" (the nonnegotiables important to him at that phase of his life) and "nice to haves" (things he could be flexible about). Initially he resisted, thinking he could process everything in his head. I encouraged him to take a day to think. When he returned a few days later, he was eager to share his decision. By making the list and clearly seeing what he'd written, he could articulate his thoughts with his mentors and trusted advisors. After good conversations, he was clear on his choice. He took the new role because he didn't yet have a family and was excited about learning something new. Since he was staying within the same company, he felt he still had a safety net. We then started preparing for his first 90 days in the new role and what success would look like for him. He has already been promoted again since our initial discussion two years ago.

I hope this example gives you better clarity on the thought you need to put into taking on a new role and planning to achieve success once you jump in with both feet. Authors Mary McNevin (2023) and Marc Effron (2018) lay out the best ways to focus on career planning in their articles in the *Harvard Business Review*.

When starting a new job, it's essential to keep in mind that career planning involves a strategic approach to managing your professional growth and development. This process includes four key steps.

1. Engage in self-reflection to identify your primary career goals, passions, and areas for improvement through introspection.

2. Gather feedback from superiors, mentors, and peers to uncover strengths and opportunities you might have overlooked.

3. Map out your career goals, existing skills, required skills, development activities, and potential obstacles into a coherent plan.

4. Regularly update your plan to reflect new developments and changes in your career or personal life.

This structured approach helps reduce career-related stress, increases perceived employability, and aligns your career path with your long-term aspirations.

Fitting in, the Meerkat Way

In the animal kingdom, one critical aspect of assimilation for newcomers is the formation of social groups. Certain species, like meerkats, rely on these social structures to integrate successfully with others. Meerkats are small carnivores native to southern Africa and known for their highly social behavior and complex social structure. They live in tight-knit groups called mobs or gangs, typically consisting of 10 to 30 individuals. These groups are organized into family units with dominant breeding pairs at the top of the hierarchy and subordinate members fulfilling various roles within the group.

When a new meerkat joins a group, whether it's a young meerkat reaching maturity or an outsider seeking acceptance, it must undergo a process of integration to fit into the existing social dynamics. This process involves four key aspects:

1. **Establishing relationships.** The newcomer must establish relationships with existing members of the group, particularly the dominant individuals and breeding pairs. Doing so may

involve grooming, social interactions, and displays of submission or deference to establish social bonds and reduce tension.

2. **Demonstrating value.** Newcomers must demonstrate their value to the group by contributing to group activities and cooperative behaviors. Doing this could include participating in group hunts, standing guard, caring for the young, or engaging in communal grooming rituals. By demonstrating their willingness to contribute and cooperate, newcomers earn the trust and acceptance of the group.

3. **Navigating social hierarchy.** Meerkat groups have a strict social hierarchy with dominant individuals asserting their authority over subordinates. Newcomers must navigate this hierarchy carefully, respecting the established order and deferring to higher-ranking individuals. Displaying submissive behaviors and avoiding confrontation helps newcomers integrate smoothly into the group.

4. **Learning group dynamics.** Each meerkat group has its own unique dynamics, communication signals, and social rules. Newcomers must learn and adapt to these group dynamics, including territorial boundaries, foraging strategies, and communication patterns. By observing and imitating the behaviors of established group members, newcomers can quickly assimilate into the social fabric of the group.

Just as the integration of newcomers is vital for the cohesion and survival of meerkat social groups, fitting into a new job is crucial for both personal and organizational success. In meerkat groups, newcomers gain access to the benefits of group living, such as protection from predators, cooperative foraging, and support in raising offspring, by aligning with the existing social structure. They achieve this through cooperation, communication, and mutual respect, highlighting the importance of social integration and cohesion.

Similarly, as you integrate into your new company, remember that you don't have to leave your authentic self behind. Fitting in doesn't mean abandoning your essence or mimicking the behaviors of those around you. Instead, focus on adapting to the new culture to facilitate faster assimilation and productivity.

In the professional world, balancing the dual objectives of assimilating into a new workplace while maintaining your authenticity is crucial. Striking this harmonious balance can be instrumental in achieving career success and personal fulfillment. By embracing the new culture and staying true to yourself, you can thrive in your new role and contribute meaningfully to your organization's goals. Assimilation into a new company involves learning and adapting to the existing culture and work styles of colleagues, which facilitates integration into the workplace. The ability to blend in fosters unity within a team, enabling a smoother and quicker transition into collaborative projects and the company community. Upholding personal integrity at work means being true to one's values and convictions, which encourages comfort and integrity in one's professional life.

> *Fitting in doesn't mean abandoning your essence or mimicking the behaviors of those around you. Instead, focus on adapting to the new culture to facilitate faster assimilation and productivity.*

Authenticity in the workplace can cultivate a sense of belonging and create a psychologically safe environment where one can thrive without pretense. It's possible to acclimate to the cultural norms of a new company while preserving one's authenticity, ensuring that personal values remain intact.

Authenticity in a professional setting means being sincere in interactions and contributing individual strengths and perspectives without oversharing personal details. Blending the need to integrate with the desire to remain true to oneself enhances personal well-being and job satisfaction, paving the way for a successful tenure in the new role. To make this work, you should be aware of your values and what matters to you. The best way to learn about this is during the interview process, as it will give you a better idea of not just the role but the company, too.

Authenticity in the workplace can cultivate a sense of belonging and create a psychologically safe environment where one can thrive without pretense.

Be an Information Seeker

The concept of the "information seeker" was coined by Thomas D. Wilson in his 1981 paper, "On User Studies and Information Needs." The term refers to someone who actively looks for information to satisfy a particular need or curiosity. This process involves identifying what information is required, locating potential sources, evaluating the information found, and using it effectively. Information seeking is a dynamic and iterative process, often involving multiple steps and sources.

Angela Merkel, formerly the chancellor of Germany and an information seeker, planned her first 90 days well, and experts often use her as a positive example of this. When she assumed office in 2005, Merkel undertook careful preparations and strategic planning to address the challenges facing Germany and to establish her leadership style. During her first 90 days, Merkel focused on building relationships with key stakeholders both domestically and internationally.

She engaged in extensive consultations with leaders from various political parties, business leaders, and foreign counterparts to gain insights into their perspectives and priorities. Merkel also prioritized policy initiatives aimed at addressing pressing issues such as economic reform, energy policy, and healthcare reform. She worked to foster consensus among coalition partners and stakeholders to advance her agenda and achieve tangible results. Merkel's meticulous planning and strategic approach during her first 90 days in office laid the groundwork for her long and successful tenure as chancellor of Germany, earning her praise for her leadership skills and ability to navigate complex political challenges.

As you navigate the initial days of your new role, create your own compass to guide you. This compass comes in the form of strategic questions that illuminate your path and ensure that you're aligned with the company's direction and your own career aspirations.

Questions to Ask Your Boss

- What milestones should I aim for in the first few months?
- How will we track and review progress?
- What's the best way to stay in touch and share updates?
- How do you steer the ship, and how can I best support that approach?
- What does success look like in my role, and how is that measured?

Questions to Ask Yourself

- In what ways will I contribute to the company's journey?
- What are my immediate and long-term career objectives in this role?

- What are the top priorities for my role according to my manager and team?
- What skills and knowledge do I need to excel in this position?
- Who are the key stakeholders I need to build relationships with?
- How will I measure my success in this role?
- What challenges might I face, and how can I prepare for them?

Just as you would carefully plan a hike by researching the trail, checking the weather, and packing the necessary gear, entering a new job also requires preparation. Getting answers to these questions is akin to plotting a course on a map because it helps you understand where you are, where you're headed, and how to get there efficiently. A proactive approach can make all the difference in a successful voyage in your new job. Let these questions be your guiding stars as you start any new aspect of your career.

Traditional Rituals

To integrate yourself in your new organization, you will need to understand a little more about the process and steps of integration that you will face beyond just learning about your role. To help you understand this process better, let's look at the concept of rites of passage.

The idea of rites of passage was first introduced by French ethnographer Arnold van Gennep in his 1909 (1981) book, *Les Rites de Passage*. He recognized these rituals as universal across cultures, marking key life transitions such as birth, puberty, marriage, and death. He outlined a three-part structure for these rites: separation, transition (or liminality), and incorporation. In the separation phase, individuals leave their previous status behind. The transition phase is a period of change and uncertainty, and the incorporation phase is when individuals reintegrate into society with their new status.

In the context of a newcomer in a company, the concept of rites of passage can describe the process of integration, adaptation, and socialization that new employees encounter as they transition into their new role and organizational culture. Here's how the theory of rites of passage can be understood in the context of a newcomer in a company:

- **Detachment:** This stage involves newcomers leaving behind their previous role or status and entering a period of transition. The stage can involve leaving a previous job, completing orientation or training, and physically entering the new workplace.

- **Adjustment:** In this stage, newcomers transition from their old company's identity and into their new role within the organization. They may experience feelings of uncertainty, ambiguity, and adjustment as they navigate the norms, expectations, and dynamics of the new workplace.

- **Integration:** The final stage involves newcomers fully integrating into the organizational culture, establishing relationships with colleagues, understanding the company's values and goals, and becoming proficient in their role. Newcomers become a full-fledged member of the organization, and this stage marks the successful completion of the rite of passage.

Rites of passage can take various forms in your new company, including orientation programs, mentorship initiatives, team-building activities, and formal or informal rituals that welcome new employees and facilitate their integration into the organizational community. These rites of passage serve not only to help newcomers acclimate to their new environment but also to reinforce organizational culture, values, and norms. They also provide opportunities for existing employees to welcome and support new colleagues, fostering a sense of belonging and camaraderie within the workplace. I explain more about how to utilize these opportunities in your new company to help you network, learn, and grow in Strategy #6 about company culture.

Rites of passage serve not only to help newcomers acclimate to their new environment but also to reinforce organizational culture, values, and norms.

The Grass Is Not Always Greener on the Other Side

Before you accept an offer from a new company, look through available public data to understand its culture and leadership. The websites Glassdoor, JobStreet, LinkedIn, and others share reviews from current employees, potential job candidates, and ex-employees. Visit the websites to see what employees are saying. Use your interview sessions to observe and listen for more useful information about your prospective new employer.

If you notice any red flags during your interview, take note of them. If needed, reach out to the recruiter to clarify any questions that arise. Focus on gaining information that helps you get the right answers to help decide. As an example, I had an interview call for an executive role from a well-known finance company a few years ago. The job description looked perfect for my experience and exactly what I was looking for in my next role. When I spoke to the recruiter, she sold the role to me. I started the interview process and attended seven interviews with different leaders in the organization. I gave 110% in every session and enjoyed the conversations. As I reflected and made notes after each interview, I realized that no one responded to my question about who the previous leader in this role was, what the current team looked like, and how many people would be reporting to me. Finally, in the last interview with the hiring leader, who was the head of HR, he asked me if I had any experience in laying off people and reorganizing teams. Sadly, I realized this role was being created to fire people and create various changes that the current HR leader didn't want to do himself. When the company approached me with an offer, I declined because I didn't feel I could add value.

You might read the story above and think, "Well, firing people and creating changes are both part of many jobs, so why was that an issue?" Several years earlier, an excellent coach helped me to think through my values and what would help me thrive at work. For me, taking a job to fire people was not an ideal situation aligned with my values. I'm glad I said no because, just three months later, the entire team I had interviewed with and their HR head were let go after the company was acquired by a competitor.

Here is another example where things worked out in the favor of the person looking for a new job. Larry was an IT director at a growing tech company where things were getting extremely hectic daily. When Larry sought to start a new chapter in his professional life, he looked for a role where he could focus as an individual contributor and continue learning while managing his growing family. When he interviewed for a company that had around 3,000 employees, he was sure that it would be able to provide the balance he desired. However, when the interviews started, he discovered that the working hours were all over the place. The company was ramping up and wanted to double its number of employees. He also found out that the role he was applying for was not new and that the person who had had the role had left due to health reasons. None of these situations is uncommon in organizations, but they were red flags for Larry because his focus was to balance his professional and personal lives. He decided not to take the offer, and he continued looking until he found a role where he stayed for the next seven years. There he was able to balance his family needs and enjoyed his work as he grew in the company. Today Larry is a senior director for IT at a Fortune 500 company.

Larry's story reminds me of my own experience when earlier in my career. In 2010 I started an exciting role in a growing tech company in San Francisco, just six months after my son was born. I was mesmerized with the vision, the people, and their goal to grow. My first week of orientation was something out of this world. My hiring manager painstakingly created an onboarding document that included all the key information about people, technology, and the *why* behind everything. My peers were helpful and smart. During orientation, I learned something new—that volunteering and giving back to the community could be part of an employee's purpose.

As a new employee, I was trying to learn the role, and I also was trying to figure out what it means to be a first-time parent while commuting nearly two hours each way. I was hungry to learn, grow, and take on the next chapter in my life. My energy level was high, and I took on this role knowing very well that I would be stretching my days. My wonderful husband was extremely supportive, and we both took on our new roles—mine as a mom and new employee and his as a new father—with 100% commitment.

Within six months, I was failing in both my roles. As a mother, I was unable to see my son wake up in the morning and spend time with him because I had to wake up at 5:00 to catch the 6:15 fast train. By the time I returned home, I had to take calls with my team in India to work on project deadlines. All of this meant that I was unable to spend quality time with my son most of the day. Babies that small don't have a fixed schedule. No matter how hard we tried, seeing the days go by without me getting satisfying time with my son was unfulfilling for me as a parent. Although everyone from my family pitched in, including my sister, in-laws, and friends, hearing the stories of my son's milestones from them was not the same as experiencing them myself. Although I shared my struggles of managing work and family with my then-boss, I was surprised that he was not ready to think through solutions with me to help manage the balance. His nonengagement and lack of support demotivated me, too. At work, I was unable to concentrate, and I questioned my own abilities and knowledge. No matter how hard I tried, I felt that I could not keep up with the work, my family, and my own health. I stepped out of the role that I had wanted for so long, heartbroken and thinking that I was truly not good at my job. Eventually I found roles closer to home in Silicon Valley. Leaders advocated for me because they had seen my work and results. Within just a few weeks, I was back on track and succeeding in my new role. As the years went by, I was able to grow my skill set, leadership acumen, and knowledge. What happened to my dream company, and why did I fail there?

At that time, I made an impulsive decision and decided to leave. Originally, I thought I was only leaving to spend more time with my baby and family, but, on further reflection, I realized aspects of the job had not felt right to me from the start. I was unable to process my professional failure within the first few months and, truth be told, the first few years. I had made lifelong friends in that company, and I kept in touch. However, I could not figure out what had gone wrong. Over time, the pieces of my debacle have come together through self-reflection, learning from my mentors, going through my own knowledge-building process in my PhD program, and giving myself grace. I wish someone had shared with me what I am about to share with you to make sure you consider all data points before accepting that next job offer.

My experience in that company was rocky from the time they interviewed me. I was hungry at a personal level and, though the name and brand of the company would be amazing for me, I gave in by taking on a role that wasn't a fit for my experience. At first, my idea was to get my foot in the door, let them see how good I was, and then get other roles. That was a wrong move. Getting my foot through the door meant taking on a role that was not my strength and accepting the position because the company had a great name. At the time I wasn't thinking how I'd need to be stellar in my first role to be considered for other roles. I didn't understand the company goals and how my work aligned those goals. I wish more help was given to professionals who want to grow in their careers. Because there isn't, we end up making mistakes like this that sometimes take a lot of time and effort to fix.

Marissa Morisson, the head of people at ZipRecruiter, shared with me her guidance for professionals seeking new opportunities to progress their careers. She emphasized the significance of staying engaged and detailed her personal practice of jotting down her expectations from a prospective role and questioning whether it would sustain her motivation and engagement. For Marissa, confirming this aspect is crucial before moving forward on any new professional venture. She advises that upon entering a new position, one should share the list of motivating factors with their new supervisor to foster better understanding.

In the past, I believed that my experiences were unique due to some poor choices I had made. However, as I interacted with several leaders, coached professionals, and mentored individuals in their career journeys, I discovered that many people encounter similar challenges. Consider Sarah, a recent graduate who joined a large tech company. During her initial week, she grappled with the intricate systems, unfamiliar jargon, and dynamics of the office environment. Assuming she was struggling alone, Sarah felt isolated. However, during a casual team lunch, she overheard Alex, the VP of engineering, recounting his early days. Alex candidly admitted once sending an email to the entire company instead of just his team. Sarah realized that everyone faced hurdles during onboarding and that seeking assistance was perfectly normal. She reached out to Alex to get some initial mentoring to help with her transition. Working with him and learning from his experience helped Sarah adjust in her new role more quickly.

James, a junior designer, received constructive feedback on his debut project. Initially disheartened, he believed he was the sole contributor to mistakes. Yet, during a design workshop, he met Maya, a renowned designer. Maya openly discussed how her early designs often met rejection, but she learned and improved from each critique. James grasped that feedback was essential for growth, even for seasoned professionals.

The shared experiences of new hires, whether navigating complex systems, handling feedback, or building relationships, underscore the universality of these challenges. By acknowledging common struggles and learning from others, new hires can navigate their professional journeys more effectively.

Successful onboarding transcends the confines of mere checklists and one-size-fits-all approaches. Over the past three decades, countless books and guides have explored the topic of onboarding, yet they often overlook the seismic shifts triggered by the COVID-19 pandemic. Employee work conditions have fundamentally transformed. The landscape has shifted dramatically—from traditional cubicles to remote workstations. Pre-pandemic, employees usually settled into physical office spaces, collaborating face to face with colleagues. However, the pandemic accelerated a rapid transition to remote work. Organizations grappled with this shift, and employees encountered new challenges related to isolation, work-life balance, and digital fatigue. This book discusses creating a supportive environment for workers, including remote employees, and emphasizes well-being, mental health, and effective communication. Whether you're a new hire or a seasoned professional, our goal is to ensure that you feel connected and engaged from day 1.

Beyond the C-suite, successful onboarding extends to professionals at all levels. Existing resources often focus on executive-level leaders stepping into new roles, but this book recognizes that every professional experiences transitions—whether it's a lateral move, a promotion, or a shift within the organization. The real-life stories of mid-level managers, individual contributors, and others who navigated these transitions successfully are included to help illustrate these various paths.

Successful onboarding transcends the confines of mere checklists and one-size-fits-all approaches.

Shift in Workplace Culture

In the second week of March 2020, the sun bathed our suburban neighborhood with a warm glow. I decided to take our dog for a walk, accompanied by my son and my nephew. The kids, full of boundless energy, raced ahead, their laughter echoing through the quiet streets. As we strolled along the sidewalk that led to our community park, I marveled at the tranquility. There were no other pedestrians—just us, the occasional rustling of leaves, and the distant thud of a basketball hitting the pavement. The park was nearly deserted, save for a lone child practicing free throws. The wind carried a hint of spring, and I felt a sense of calm settle over me.

These walks had become my sanctuary, a respite from the demands of daily life. The rhythm of my footsteps, the rustle of leaves underfoot, and the distant laughter of my son all contributed to my mental well-being. I vowed to make these walks a regular part of my routine. And then, just as the sun warmed my skin, my phone buzzed in my pocket. I read the urgent message: Californians were being asked to shelter at home. I immediately called my husband. Together, we puzzled over the implications. What did this order mean? Was it safe to venture outside?

I gathered the kids and our dog, and we rushed back home. The usual 10-minute walk stretched longer as I paused repeatedly to read group WhatsApp messages from concerned friends and family. The gravity of the situation sank in: COVID-19 had swept across the globe. Governments and companies alike were urging employees to work remotely. Who could have foreseen that this moment would mark the beginning of a seismic shift in the world of work? Remote work became the new norm, blurring the boundaries between office and home and forever altering the trajectory of our careers. Days were much longer as we didn't manage when work stopped for the day. Working parents moved from their computer screens to their children's homework while cooking all the meals and taking care of every aspect of their homes (now also their home office), which made the days longer and tough to manage.

The outbreak of the COVID-19 pandemic unleashed a wave of unprecedented changes across societies worldwide, profoundly altering the landscape of work and employment. From remote work to heightened health concerns, the pandemic has reshaped the situation for employees in ways previously unimaginable. The impacts of COVID-19 on employees included shifts in work arrangements, mental health challenges, and the evolving employer-employee relationship.

Remote and Hybrid Work Revolution

One of the most notable transformations in the wake of COVID-19 has been the widespread adoption of remote work. Overnight, companies across industries transitioned their operations online to mitigate the spread of the virus. What began as a temporary measure evolved into a seismic shift in how work is conducted. Employees now have greater flexibility in managing their time and location, blurring the boundaries between work and personal life. Although remote work offers newfound freedom, it also presents challenges such as isolation, digital fatigue, and difficulties in maintaining work-life balance.

> *Employees now have greater flexibility in managing their time and location, blurring the boundaries between work and personal life.*

Redefining the Employer-Employee Relationship

COVID-19 has prompted a reevaluation of the traditional employer-employee relationship. With remote work becoming the norm, the dynamics of supervision and collaboration have undergone significant changes. Managers are learning to trust employees to deliver results without constant oversight, emphasizing outcomes over hours worked. This shift toward a more results-oriented approach has paved the way for greater autonomy and empowerment among employees. Additionally, the pandemic highlighted the importance of empathy and compassion in leadership, as employers strive to support their teams through challenging times.

Economic Uncertainty

The economic fallout of the pandemic led to widespread job losses, furloughs, and financial insecurity for many employees. Hospitality, tourism, and retail industries have been particularly hard hit, leaving millions unemployed or underemployed. The gig economy has also faced challenges, with gig workers experiencing fluctuations in demand and income instability. This economic fallout was hardest toward the end of 2023 and the first half of 2024, when we saw layoffs in thousands across different sectors and companies globally. As the economy comes back to a balance, we will see a rise in new roles and new organizations (through mergers and acquisitions), and we will see roles emerge with the advent of artificial intelligence in the marketplace.

You, as a new hire, find yourself navigating a landscape transformed due to the COVID-19 pandemic. Traditional work norms have shifted, giving rise to remote work arrangements, mental health considerations, and evolving relationships between employers and employees. The flexibility of remote work is a boon that also brings challenges like isolation and burnout. As we grapple with the ongoing effects of the pandemic, recognize the importance of adaptability and resilience. The dynamics of work are in flux, and your ability to adjust and stay resilient will be crucial.

What Type of Employee Are You?

In my first corporate job, all new hires had to attend a one-week in-person bootcamp. Leaders focused on cultural aspects of the company and on safety issues, compliance sessions, and the like. Due to the bootcamp, I felt well connected to the company and the cohort that started with me. I understood the large company campus well by the end of that week. Things have changed drastically since then. New-hire onboarding sessions are getting shorter and, in some companies, they are done in a hybrid manner (in-person and virtual) or they are completely virtual. If you are a new college graduate joining the workforce, doing your onboarding virtually might not be a big deal for you after years of online school. For those more experienced workers, this change might be difficult to handle. Jeffrey, a software engineer, had been with his company for 15 years, starting right after he graduated from college. When he began that job, the onboarding

23

was in person and a three-day session. When he changed jobs, his onboarding was not what he expected. He was asked to join a virtual session. The laptop and anything else that he needed was shipped to his home. He'd be able to go into the nearest office once a week, but it wasn't required. Suddenly he moved from being a full-time, on-site employee to a completely remote employee. Unfortunately, the first three months were very tough, as Jeffrey didn't realize how much he would miss being on-site with colleagues. Even the communication with his manager, who was in a different time zone, was not going well. He didn't feel connected to the company or his colleagues and felt he was being ignored. In his previous company, whenever there was a group meeting, everyone would gather in a room, catch up, and provide project updates. Usually this would lead to further networking and relationship building with colleagues. Now everyone was taking calls from home. In these calls, some people didn't have their cameras on; others walked around and shook their phone camera. Jeffrey found this distracting, and it added to his challenges around connecting with his colleagues.

He realized he needed to change his style of working or find a different job. He sought help from friends who worked in fully remote positions and learned ways of working and managing his virtual relationships with peers and his boss and was able to pivot quickly. Not everyone has the capacity to change in this way. The next sections explain some ways to identify what type of employee you are and the best way to manage your workday as you transition into your new role.

Remote Workers

A remote employee is an individual who performs regular work duties off company property and is removed from direct contact with managers or supervisors.

Some of the challenges remote workers face are described next.

- **Feeling isolated.** Remote work often leads to feelings of isolation. Without the daily interactions that come with a physical office, employees may miss out on casual conversations, team lunches, and impromptu brainstorming sessions. To combat these feelings, regular virtual team-building activities, video calls, and social interactions help foster a sense of belonging and maintain team cohesion.

- **Managing boundaries.** The lack of clear boundaries between work and personal life is another challenge. When your home doubles as your office, work hours can easily spill into evenings or weekends. Setting a dedicated workspace and adhering to a schedule can help maintain a healthy balance. Designate specific work hours, take breaks, and create physical and mental boundaries to prevent burnout.

- **Communication challenges.** Remote employees rely on digital communication tools—email, chat, video calls—to collaborate with colleagues. However, miscommunication can occur due to the absence of face-to-face interactions. Clear communication channels, responsive colleagues, and well-defined processes are crucial. Regular check-ins, status updates, and project management tools help bridge the gap and keep everyone aligned. The way to avoid these issues is to plan, be ready for change, and have ongoing communication with your hiring manager to discuss the best way to manage your transition.

Remote work offers numerous benefits for both employers and employees. Employees enjoy the flexibility to create a customized work environment that suits their needs, leading to increased productivity as they can focus without the distractions of a busy office.

This setup allows them to structure their day to optimize energy levels and deliver high-quality work. Employers benefit from significant cost savings on office space, utilities, and facilities management. With remote work, they can attract a wider talent pool since geographical constraints are no longer a barrier to recruitment. Additionally, remote work enables employees to better manage family commitments, personal interests, and overall well-being, promoting a healthier work-life balance.

A Day in the Life of a Remote Worker: Priyanka

Priyanka, a marketing specialist, works remotely for a tech startup. She starts her day with a virtual team huddle via video conferencing, where the team discusses goals, priorities, and upcoming campaigns. Throughout her remote workday, Priyanka uses project management tools like Trello and Slack to stay connected with colleagues, ensuring alignment and progress through regular check-ins. Video calls with the design team allow her to provide feedback on creatives for an upcoming product launch, and the team utilizes whiteboard features in their video call platform to brainstorm and plan next steps.

The absence of office distractions helps Priyanka focus deeply. Between meetings, she collaborates with the content team on a blog post about the latest software update. She wraps up tasks, sends a status update to the team, and logs off at the end of the day. Thanks to no commute, Priyanka can be more productive, but this is possible only because she meticulously plans her day and week. Her regular communication with her team and boss, along with detailed project updates, ensures everyone stays on the same page and can track her progress effectively.

Hybrid Workers

Hybrid work is a flexible model that supports a blend of in-office and remote employees. This approach offers employees the autonomy to choose where and how they work based on their productivity and preferences. If hybrid work is mentioned in your discussion for your new job, be sure to clarify with your hiring manager or recruiter how the new company defines "hybrid." Several types of this work model exist.

- **Flexible hybrid model.** Employees choose their location and working hours based on daily priorities. They can work from home or go into the office as needed.

- **Fixed hybrid model.** Organizations set specific days and times for remote work and in-office presence.

- **Hub-and-spoke model.** Companies maintain a central office (hub) while allowing employees to work from smaller satellite locations (spokes).

- **Hoteling model.** Employees reserve office space when needed, promoting flexibility and efficient space utilization.

A Day in the Life of a Hybrid Software Engineer: John

John starts his day at 7:00 am with a morning routine that includes breakfast and a quick workout. By 8:00, he logs into the company's virtual workspace from home, checks emails, and reviews his schedule. At 9:00, he joins a virtual team meeting to discuss ongoing projects and set goals for the day.

(continued)

(continued)

After a lunch break at noon, John heads to the office at 1:00 pm, using the commute to catch up on industry podcasts. He arrives at the office by 2:00 and participates in a brainstorming session with colleagues, which helps spark new ideas and fosters collaboration. The afternoon is spent working on individual tasks that require focus, taking advantage of the office's quiet spaces.

At 5:00 pm, John wraps up his day with a quick check-in with his manager to discuss progress and any roadblocks. He heads home at 6:00 using the commute to unwind and transition out of work mode. By 7:00 pm, John is home, enjoying dinner and leisure time with family or friends. This hybrid schedule allows John to balance focused work at home with collaborative efforts in the office, enhancing his productivity and job satisfaction.

Full-Time On-Site Employees

Before the advent of COVID in our world, I had never had a full-time remote job. I did have hybrid options, but most of my professional career was spent as an on-site, full-time employee. As the world changed around us and brought significantly different working options, it organizations were forced to adjust to these changes. Depending on which phase of life you are in (recent graduate, caretaker, dealing with health issues, etc.), working on-site might require a lot more effort from your side. Whatever your preferences are, we are lucky to be able to build a career during this new revolution in work. To understand how companies today are defining on-site employees, read the next definitions of work types from three global companies.

Korn Ferry characterizes a full-time on-site employee as someone who works primarily at the employer's physical location. (This contrasts with remote or hybrid work models, where employees divide their time between home and the office.) On-site employees are expected to be present during regular business hours, performing their tasks and responsibilities on-site.

PwC defines full-time on-site employees as those who spend most of their work hours at a client site, PwC office, or other in-person locations. This model supports the business's in-office needs, providing essential on-site technology services or critical in-person support. PwC stresses the importance of physical presence to foster collaboration and meet client engagement requirements.

Accenture describes a full-time on-site employee as someone who is present at the workplace for the majority of the workweek, engaging with clients and colleagues in person and prioritizing face-to-face meetings and collaboration. Accenture promotes in-person interactions to build strong professional relationships and boost productivity.

Working on-site provides numerous benefits compared to remote work. It enables direct collaboration and communication with colleagues, which can improve teamwork and strengthen company culture. Being in the office allows for spontaneous interactions and immediate feedback, leading to faster problem-solving and innovation. On-site work also grants access to resources and equipment that might not be available at home, ensuring employees can perform their tasks effectively. Furthermore, the structured office environment helps maintain a clear distinction between work and personal life, promoting better work-life balance and overall productivity.

After accepting a new job offer, it's crucial to clearly understand your employer's expectations and how it defines different types of employees. Each company may have varying definitions; for instance, you might be considered a remote employee but still be required to travel to a central location quarterly for team meetings or business reviews. As a hybrid employee, you may need to work on-site each week or month for a specified number of hours. To avoid any misunderstandings, ensure these details are explicitly stated in your offer letter or confirmed via email with your recruiter or hiring manager. This clarity will help reduce stress and confusion, allowing you to focus on onboarding smoothly and mastering your new role.

Proven Strategies to Plan Your Success

No matter what type of employee you are, you will need to create a strong plan with achievable milestones to be successful fast. As I was researching this book, I decided to focus on seven strategies, because this number holds a unique and significant value in cultures, religions, and the modern world. Examples of seven as a lucky number are abundant in the world around us. The ancient and modern lists of the Seven Wonders of the World include awe-inspiring structures that symbolize completeness and perfection. The seven colors of the rainbow are seen as a symbol of hope and promise. In music, seven notes form the foundation of Western music. Additionally, the seven-day week is a global standard, reflecting the ancient belief in the significance of the number 7.

Mathematically, 7 stands out among the first 10 numbers because it cannot be evenly divided or multiplied to yield another whole number within this range. This distinctiveness adds to its allure and intrigue. Moreover, research indicates that people generally prefer odd numbers over even ones, with 7 frequently emerging as a favorite. Overall, the historical, cultural, and mathematical significance of the number 7 contributes to its reputation as a lucky number. Its presence in various aspects of life and its unique properties make it a symbol of good fortune and completeness. We know the saying "Luck favors the brave," so this book gives you an opportunity to be prepared and take your hard work forward. Here are the seven strategies you need to focus on to create a proactive plan to take charge of your success. Each strategy is explained in its own chapter with examples, tools, and actionable ideas.

Strategy #1: People

Research has shown that by building strong relationships at work, newcomers can assimilate faster into their new roles and companies. In this chapter, I show you how to do just that. In a new role, you will be drinking from the fire hose, so you must be prepared and take good notes. Read through Strategy #1 to lay a strong foundation and start your new role on the right foot. If you do this part well, everything else will fall in place.

Strategy #2: Goal Setting and Feedback

When joining a company, people often face a whirlwind of information, tasks, and expectations. Setting clear goals provides you with a sense of direction and purpose. Knowing what is expected of you allows you to focus your efforts effectively. These goals serve as powerful motivators, driving engagement and commitment. This chapter addresses constructive feedback, which highlights areas where new hires can grow and provides actionable insights, allowing individuals to make necessary adjustments. Feedback exchanges foster stronger relationships between new hires and their managers or colleagues. By creating an open communication channel, feedback contributes to a supportive work environment where growth and development thrive.

Knowing what is expected of you allows you to focus your efforts effectively.

Strategy #3: Company Processes

Company processes help to fuel decision making and help employees collaborate. The larger the company, the more processes you should expect. Medical services, biotechnology, manufacturing, banking, and many others have strict processes in place. To be successful in your new role in such industries, you should spend as much time as possible learning the processes. In this chapter, I help you decipher the different types of processes you might need to learn and the best way to design your learning based on your role.

Strategy #4: Navigating Technology in Your New Role

Navigating technology as a new hire in a company can be challenging but manageable with the right approach. This strategy shares how new hires should familiarize themselves with the company's digital tools and resources, including email systems and project management tools. Taking advantage of training sessions and onboarding programs is essential. Building a network within the company, such as connecting with IT support and experienced colleagues, can provide valuable guidance. This strategy is important because it will help you prioritize and learn fast as you transition from a new hire to a productive team member.

Strategy #5: Know the Business

Know what the overall ecosystem is of running the business internally and externally in the company. This chapter is especially important for new college graduates who will be joining the corporate world and for those with mid-level experience. Usually anyone with over 10 years of experience in the industry has a good idea of the business, but this chapter can be used as a good refresher, too.

Strategy #6: The Company Culture

This chapter provides a simplified version of what culture in a company looks like, how to observe and learn about it, and how you can use the culture to boost your productivity. The word "culture" has been used in many ways in industry and popular media. During the COVID era, the word was used to highlight how companies were taking care of their employees during the tough times, including layoffs and remote work versus on-site work.

Strategy #7: Keep Learning

All the leaders and employees I interviewed mentioned this one skill as helping them to assimilate faster in their roles and companies. Continuous learning helped them to scale better career heights.

These seven strategies will help you to plan, evaluate, and course correct your direction in this new phase of your life.

People

*Understanding people affects your ability to communicate
with others.*

—John Ford

STEVE HAD BEEN A SALES leader for 15 years. He had been
successful in his last role and had received several accolades
in his last company. His organization went through a reorganiza-
tion recently, and he didn't enjoy reporting to his new boss. This
made him eager to explore the market, and he started responding to
the LinkedIn recruiters reaching out to him. After several interviews,
rethinking whether he was making the right decision, going through
the guilt complex, and working through a highly negotiated salary
package, Steve received his new job offer. Steve was thrilled to leave
his old company and boss.

In the negotiated package, he requested to join a few weeks later
since he figured he might as well get a good break, get rejuvenated,
and prepare for his new role. These were good ideas, but the problem was Steve did not take that time to plan. He showed up on the
first day of work, finished his HR orientation, met with his boss, and
expected the first few weeks to be the honeymoon phase. He was
wrong.

After the half-day orientation, his manager took him to lunch,
which was only 30 minutes long, and invited him to a series of meetings. In these meetings, Steve met many new colleagues, learned

customer names, shook hands in person, and virtually met with many more people in the company. He was overwhelmed and could not keep up with the information overflow. By the end of the week, Steve was confused, tired, and didn't feel ready to return to his new role. The next week, he was not confident and appeared defensive in several meetings. At the end of his first 30 days, his manager pulled him aside and delivered disappointing feedback. In those early days, Steve kept on taking the punches and couldn't learn fast enough because he didn't focus on the most crucial part of his new job: his first 30 days. Eventually, Steve left his new role and decided to return to his old company. He had learned his lesson. This time around at his old employer, where he was lucky to get his old job back, he decided to create a strong plan.

Tom Brady, now an NFL icon, was chosen as the 199th pick in the draft's sixth round by the New England Patriots in 2000. He began as a lowly fourth-string quarterback. Yet his resolve to excel was unwavering. He dedicated innumerable hours to mastering the team's playbook, dissecting opponent defenses, and grasping intricate game plans. This rigorous discipline and indefatigable dedication bore fruit when an injury to the first-string quarterback presented him with an unexpected opportunity. Brady grasped this chance with both hands and transformed the unexpected opportunity into a legacy. His commitment to thorough preparation manifested in stellar on-field performances, propelling the Patriots to their inaugural Super Bowl win in the 2001 season, followed by six more titles under Brady's leadership. Brady's triumphs stemmed not only from his athletic prowess but also from his strategic acumen and leadership finesse.

His journey didn't end there. Upon joining the Tampa Bay Buccaneers in 2020, Brady's ethos of diligent preparation remained his guiding principle. In his first season, he guided the Buccaneers to Super Bowl glory, demonstrating that, with persistent effort and strategic foresight, one can achieve greatness even amid new challenges. Brady's illustrious career stands as a powerful testament to the notion that success is defined not by your starting point but by the dedication and strategy you apply along the way.

The moment you receive a job offer, it's time to put pen to paper and begin charting your path to success in your new role. Whether you're transitioning from another position and company, freshly graduated and eager for your first job, or returning from a career break, the company expects you to arrive well prepared and ready to dive in. Without a thoughtful plan, your experience could resemble Steve's—lacking direction and failing to prioritize the critical aspects of your role.

Brandon Carson, who served as the head of global learning, leadership, and cultural experiences at Starbucks, has an impressive track record in learning and development. His experience includes leadership roles at companies such as Walmart, Delta, Microsoft, and Yahoo. During my research for the book, I had the privilege of speaking with him shortly after he assumed his position at Starbucks. This conversation provided valuable insights into the key factors behind his long-standing success. When I asked him about his top priority when joining a new role, his response was unwavering: people.

Carson recognizes that investing in people is fundamental to achieving organizational excellence. He says:

> I call it the human system. At the end of the day, the work as an executive revolves around human connection. Some cultures value it more than others, but to succeed in this era of disruption, disinformation, and division, we all place a high value on building the connections that will bring measurable impact.

According to Carson, in any organization, especially those with many employees spread in different locations, it can take a year just to make strong connections. You need to accelerate your impact through intentional and diligent planning.

Carson's experience reflects the distinct phases that newcomers usually go through when joining a new company or starting a new job. Let's talk about a few of these phases.

Navigating the New

Embracing a learning mindset and remaining open to new experiences lay the foundation for a successful transition.

The first days and weeks at a new job are characterized by a mix of anticipation and adjustment. As newcomers navigate unfamiliar surroundings and procedures, they may experience a range of emotions—from excitement to apprehension. Establishing a routine, familiarizing oneself with company culture and expectations, and seeking guidance from colleagues and mentors are essential steps in the process of adaptation. Embracing a learning mindset and remaining open to new experiences lay the foundation for a successful transition.

Investing time and effort in nurturing meaningful connections contributes not only to personal growth but also to the overall success of the team and organization.

Building Relationships

Building rapport, demonstrating initiative, and actively participating in team activities foster a sense of belonging and integration within the organization. Networking both within and outside the immediate team facilitates collaboration, knowledge sharing, and professional development opportunities. Investing time and effort in nurturing meaningful connections contributes not only to personal growth but also to the overall success of the team and organization.

Overcoming Obstacles with Resilience

Although joining a new job is an exciting prospect, it is not without its challenges. From mastering new skills to adapting to organizational dynamics, newcomers may encounter obstacles along the way. Imposter syndrome, the fear of failure, and the pressure to perform can undermine confidence and hinder progress. However, resilience, perseverance, and a positive attitude are invaluable assets in overcoming setbacks and navigating challenges. Seeking support from colleagues, leveraging resources provided by the organization, and maintaining a growth mindset empower individuals to overcome adversity and thrive in their new roles.

Embracing Opportunities

Joining a new job presents opportunities for personal and professional growth. From access to training programs and mentorship initiatives to exposure to diverse projects and responsibilities, newcomers have the chance to expand their skills, broaden their knowledge, and advance their careers. Embracing opportunities for continuous learning, taking on new challenges, and seizing moments of innovation contribute to individual development and organizational success. By approaching growth and development proactively, individuals can maximize their potential and make meaningful contributions to their teams and the broader organization.

Joining a new job is a transformative journey that encompasses anticipation, adjustment, relationship building, overcoming challenges, and embracing opportunities for growth and development. By navigating the initial phase with resilience, building meaningful connections, and seizing opportunities for learning and advancement, newcomers can start on a path of success and fulfillment in their new roles. As one embraces the challenges and rewards that come with joining a new job, one contributes to the vibrant tapestry of talent and innovation within the organization, driving progress and prosperity for oneself and the company.

Let's look at an example of one of the youngest political leaders and how she successfully built her brand and objectives with a strong team. Jacinda Ardern assumed the role of prime minister of New Zealand on October 26, 2017, becoming the nation's youngest prime minister in over 150 years at the age of 37. Leading the Labour Party, she swiftly gained recognition for her empathetic and decisive approach to leadership. She created a carefully planned brand strategy with her leadership team to develop impactful programs for the communities she served.

When she became the prime minister, she took several strategic actions to set the tone for her leadership and address the country's pressing issues. In her first 90 days, she built a strong and diverse team by appointing key ministers who shared her commitment to social justice, economic fairness, and environmental sustainability, such as Grant Robertson as finance minister and David Parker as environment minister. Ardern also set clear goals through her 100-Day Plan, focusing on immediate and impactful changes. These goals included introducing a bill to halve child poverty and improve child well-being, launching the KiwiBuild program to construct 100,000 affordable homes over 10 years, setting a goal for New Zealand to be carbon neutral by 2050 with the establishment of a Climate Commission, and passing the Healthy Homes Guarantee Bill to ensure rental properties met minimum standards for warmth and dryness, alongside introducing the Families Package to increase incomes and reduce child poverty.

Additionally, Ardern's government shifted its focus toward long-term sustainability and social equity by implementing tax reforms and incentives to stimulate economic growth while ensuring fairness, announcing free post-secondary education for the first year starting in 2018 to make higher education more accessible, and introducing changes to employment law to bring greater fairness to the workplace, including extending paid parental leave and increasing the minimum wage. She emphasized transparency and direct communication with the public by holding regular press conferences and using social media to engage with citizens, ensuring they were informed and involved in the government's initiatives.

Beyond the 100 days, Ardern's leadership during crises, such as the Christchurch mosque attacks and the COVID-19 pandemic, further demonstrated her ability to lead with empathy and decisiveness, reinforcing her commitment to protecting and uniting the nation. Ardern's proactive and compassionate approach in her first 100 days set the foundation for her tenure and demonstrated her commitment to creating a more inclusive and sustainable New Zealand. She has been globally recognized as an action-oriented, empathetic leader.

Starting a new role is akin to setting sail on a voyage where the connections you forge are as vital as the compass guiding your path. In the realm of work, relationships are the sinews that bind the fabric of an organization together, fostering a sense of belonging and purpose. As a new hire, establishing rapport with colleagues is a strategic step that can propel your career forward. Through these connections, you gain insights into the company's heartbeat: the unspoken rules, the shared triumphs, and the collective challenges. Knowing who your stakeholders are, understanding their expectations, and investing time in nurturing these relationships can unlock doors to collaboration, mentorship, and opportunities that might otherwise remain closed. In essence, building relationships is the cornerstone of not just surviving but thriving in your new job because the people around you will be your allies.

Lori Beer, chief information officer at JPMorgan Chase, and Richard Branson, founder of the Virgin Group, both emphasize the critical role of collaborative relationships in achieving business success. Beer underscores the necessity of teamwork both within the company and with external partners to deliver winning outcomes for customers, asserting that while technical acumen is valuable, the constructive collaboration created through cooperation and a deep understanding of technology's impact on service delivery is indispensable. Similarly, Branson champions the idea that the essence of business triumph lies in personal connections, suggesting that the caliber of these relationships is fundamental to the prosperity or failure of any business endeavor. Together, their insights convey a powerful message: Building strong relationships is not just beneficial but essential for long-term success in the business world.

When you start your new role, be ready with a plan that focuses on meeting the people listed in the stakeholder section in this chapter. Your goal is to learn about them, their role, what is working well, what opportunities lie ahead and how you can work with them in a successful way.

Your Work Location Matters

In the introduction, we walked through how the world has changed after COVID and how that has impacted work models. Barely any options of working from home existed when I started my career. We had to show up on-site for our new jobs, go through all the onboarding and orientation paperwork, and find our desk or cubicle, and all of that took place in person. Over the years, we saw a progression toward using online tools. Several startups and global organizations relied on these tools for more than 90% of their work. Many industries observed the adoption yet stayed in their comfortable space of not using these tools to maximize their utility.

Years ago, I was invited for a job interview at a global organization that was a big name in the tech industry. The process was smooth, and I was enjoying learning about the company, the culture, and the key role. In this process, the recruiter called me directly on my phone for all the discussions. Then we progressed to talking to the hiring manager. In the invite, they sent me a Zoom call link and the date/time. I was excited to talk to the hiring manager. That morning, I made sure I was dressed my best to be ready for the video interview. The interview started, and I adjusted my video and started the discussion. After a few minutes of meet and greet, I politely asked the hiring manager if he would be joining the video call. He said, "This is a phone interview, and we won't need the video." His response surprised me. I was silent for a few seconds and responded with "okay."

I am sure you are thinking the same thing I was thinking: "Why not just have a call over the phone instead of sending a Zoom link?" For me, sending a Zoom link meant that we were meeting by video. I learned fast that the members of the company felt more comfortable with audio tools even though they had access to communication software tools like Zoom.

As the interview conversation continued and we jumped into the technical aspects of the discussion, the hiring manager wanted to meet up in person. He asked me to use the company shuttle to meet him at the company headquarters, which was in a different state. I was five states away, and I was confused when he said that. In my mind, I thought that taking the shuttle would require a few days of travel. He heard the long silence at my end and rephrased his statement. He said, "Why don't you take the company plane available to senior leaders from your city and meet our team at headquarters?" You can imagine my embarrassment, and I was glad that we didn't have the video on for this conversation. I replied that I'd love to do that. Even though I made a few minor mistakes since this company was so different, I still got the job offer.

I am sharing this story as a reminder that it's wise to understand how the people inside an organization use their tools and resources. From this story, we can see that not everyone will adopt the entirety of a technological tool, even when they're available. And whereas most companies don't have their own company planes, this one did, and it was okay for leaders to use it for employee meetings. Once you're hired, these are the types of things that are important to learn about so you know the best ways to communicate.

Another example was the logic of using instant messaging (IM), such as Slack or MS Teams, to communicate. One organization I worked for frowned on using IM if you were within walking distance of those you were messaging. Yet if you had a question and were in a different location from your team or boss, using IM was acceptable. Every company has different expectations. Taking the culturally "correct" steps in each situation will show you can work well with others inside the team and company. We explore this aspect of communication tools later in the book with examples and different ways of learning the best way to utilize the tools as per company policies and expectations.

Succeeding as an On-Site or In-Person Employee

Being productive as an on-site or in-person employee involves different considerations compared to remote work. Strategies to maximize productivity while working at a physical office are listed next.

- **Arrive early and manage your workspace.** Reach the office on time to kickstart your day with a high level of inspiration, a positive mindset, and a hunger to learn everything you need about your job. Make sure to arrange your desk, organize materials, and ensure everything you need is within reach. Although I'm a minimalist at my work desks, I always surround myself with inspiring books and articles. Having these materials displayed has provided great ice breakers with colleagues. When they see interesting book titles at my desk and ask about them, I can offer to let them borrow the books.

This is a useful way to develop strong colleague connections.

- **Prioritize your tasks.** Chances are you will have to take several new hire and onboarding training courses. Begin your day by reviewing your tasks, and do your best to manage your day so that you can plan for the time you need to spend on any training courses. Prioritize based on urgency (do you need to complete something immediately?) and importance. Address any doubts or concerns with your manager and see if he or she can help you to prioritize.

- **Use effective in-person communication.** Observe how your team operates so you can adjust your communication style based on their preferences. When in doubt, ask your colleagues the best way to connect with them since you will have a lot of questions during your first 100 days. For example, you might visit a colleague's desk for quick discussions instead of relying solely on emails or chat. However, you want to be sure in advance that your colleague will appreciate in-person and informal approaches.

- **Minimize distractions.** Keep personal calls and social media browsing to a minimum. If you sit in a cubicle area, step away from your desk and take any calls elsewhere. If possible, keep your phone on silent mode. Although breaks are essential, ensure they don't disrupt your workflow.

- **Collaborate and network.** Brainstorm, collaborate, and share ideas. Building your professional relationships will help you to find answers faster and enhance your productivity.

- **Engage in healthy habits.** Do your best to stay hydrated by keeping a water bottle at your desk and controlling the amount of caffeine you consume. Caffeine will give you energy for a short time, but you will feel a crash later. At lunchtime, take a break and have lunch with your colleagues. Early in my career I spent a lot of time during lunch trying to finish up tasks, but I missed meeting my peers and creating relationships with them. I also overworked and exhausted myself since I would not take regular breaks. Knowing your limit and what energizes you will help you to have productive days.

Succeeding as a Remote Employee

As a remote employee, you can use the next practical tips to enhance your productivity and maintain a healthy work-life balance.

- **Create a dedicated workspace.** Designate a separate area in your home specifically for work. This physical separation helps you mentally switch between your work and your personal lives. When you step into your workspace, you know it's time to focus on work.

- **Set clear goals and use to-do lists.** Define daily goals and create a to-do list. Prioritize tasks and break them down into manageable steps. Doing this keeps you organized and motivated during the day.

- **Stick to a schedule.** Establish a consistent work routine. Set specific working hours and adhere to them. Having a predictable schedule helps maintain discipline and work-life boundaries.

- **Minimize distractions.** Identify potential distractions and address them. Turn off notifications, close unnecessary tabs, and create a quiet environment. Consider using noise-canceling headphones.

- **Take frequent breaks.** Regular breaks improve focus and prevent burnout. Use techniques like the Pomodoro method, developed by Francesco Cirillo 30 years ago as a time management technique to maintain productivity. The method involves breaking work time into 25-minute focused sessions, followed by 5-minute breaks, optimizing productivity while minimizing interruptions.

- **Leverage productivity software.** Use tools that enhance efficiency. Consider project management apps, time-tracking software, and communication platforms to streamline your work.

Identify Your Key Stakeholders

In my early years, when I first joined a company, no one taught me that people working in a group environment are answerable to more than just their direct boss. When I worked in the human resources function, for example, I was answerable not just to my direct boss but also to functional leaders, business partners, and any cross-functional leaders whom I worked with. This was because I was in a central or corporate role, where the main goal was to provide HR service to functional leaders across the globe in different teams. When I worked in sales and marketing, it was easier to understand my scope and my stakeholders since my role was within a functional group and not in a service role in the center of the company. Typical key stakeholders are described next.

Direct Supervisor

Your immediate supervisor or manager is one of your primary stakeholders. This person provides guidance, direction, and feedback on your work performance and plays a significant role in your day-to-day responsibilities and professional development. In one of my first corporate jobs, I worked with several stakeholders. This distracted me, and I didn't realize that understanding my supervisor's goals was the biggest way to measure my success. Due to the distraction, I missed communicating on a regular basis with my supervisor. Even though I worked hard to support my stakeholder's goals, my direct supervisor and I were not on the same page. In Strategy #2, I provide tools and insights on the best way to plan and manage your relationship with your manager.

Colleagues and Peers

Your colleagues and peers within your team or department play a crucial role as stakeholders. In the course of my research, I conducted interviews with several newcomers across various functions and experience levels. Remarkably, their responses consistently highlighted the same key factor in successful assimilation into a new role: the importance of peers and coworkers, whose influence was second only to that of their direct supervisor. These colleagues collaborate with you on projects, generously share knowledge and expertise, and significantly contribute to the overall success of the team. Cultivating positive relationships with your coworkers fosters a supportive and collaborative work environment.

Senior Leadership

Senior leaders and executives within the organization influence strategic direction, organizational culture, and decision making. Although you may not interact with them directly daily, their vision, priorities, and expectations shape the broader context in which you work.

Cross-Functional Teams

You may work with individuals from other departments or functional areas on cross-functional teams or projects. These stakeholders may include representatives from marketing, sales, finance, human resources, or operations. Collaborating effectively with cross-functional teams requires communication, alignment, and coordination.

Clients or Customers

This discussion applies to you only if your role involves directly serving clients or customers. They impact the success of your work and the organization. Understanding their needs, preferences, and expectations is essential for delivering value and building strong client relationships.

Suppliers and Vendors

If your work involves procurement or supply chain management, suppliers and vendors are stakeholders who provide goods or services essential for the organization's operations. Building positive relationships with suppliers and vendors is important for ensuring quality, reliability, and cost effectiveness.

Regulatory Bodies and Government Agencies

Depending on the industry and nature of the organization, regulatory bodies, government agencies, or industry associations may be stakeholders who influence compliance requirements, industry standards, and regulatory frameworks.

Shareholders or Investors

Shareholders or investors who have a financial stake in the company may influence strategic decisions, financial performance, and corporate governance. Their interests may include profitability, growth, sustainability, and corporate social responsibility.

Community and Society

The broader community and society in which the organization operates are stakeholders who may be affected by its actions, policies, and practices. This constituency includes local communities, nonprofit organizations, advocacy groups, and other stakeholders who have an interest in the organization's social and environmental impact.

Yourself

Last but not least, *you* are a stakeholder in your own success and well-being within the organization. Understanding your own goals, values, and aspirations is essential for aligning your work with your personal and professional objectives.

Identifying and understanding your stakeholders allows you to navigate relationships, manage expectations, and collaborate effectively to achieve common goals and drive success within the organization. Early planning is a wise step given the number of stakeholders you might encounter in your new role.

How to Identify and Map Your Stakeholders

Stakeholder mapping is a process of creating a visual representation of the people or organizations involved in or affected by a project, product, or idea. The map helps to identify and analyze their interests, influence, and importance in relation to the project. Stakeholder mapping can help you to communicate effectively with your stakeholders, manage their expectations, and gain their support for your project.

Although there are various ways to create a stakeholder map, a common approach is to use a four-quadrant matrix, first developed by Aubrey L. Mendelow, a professor of management and information systems at the Graduate School of Management at Kent State University. The four-quadrant approach, or Mendelow's Matrix, also known as the Power-Interest Grid, is a tool used in stakeholder management to categorize stakeholders based on their level of interest in a project and their power to influence it. This matrix helps project managers and leaders prioritize their engagement strategies with different stakeholders. The four quadrants in the matrix are shown in Exhibit 1.1 and discussed in the next paragraphs.

Exhibit 1.1 Stakeholder Map

Key Influencers	*Supportive Advocates*
(High Interest, High Influence)	(High Interest, Low Influence)
Powerful Observers	*Casual Bystanders*
(Low Interest, High Influence)	(Low Interest, Low Influence)

1. **Key Influencers (High Interest, High Influence),** at the top left of the matrix, are stakeholders with significant power and interest in the project, often including decision makers, sponsors, or leaders who can greatly impact the project's success or failure. Engaging with them actively and keeping them satisfied and well informed is essential throughout the project. In my conversations with leaders, this style of communication emerged as a focal point, recognized as a crucial factor in both individual and leadership success.

Depending on your company's culture, your boss's expectations, and the reporting hierarchy, you might need to update a single key influencer or a larger group. Engage in an open and honest conversation with your boss to pinpoint key influencers. This understanding may shift based on the projects you undertake, and doing this simple exercise will help you align effectively with expectations.

2. **Supportive Advocates (High Interest, Low Influence),** at the top right of the matrix, are stakeholders who are highly interested in the project but lack the power to influence it significantly. They often include end users, customers, or beneficiaries. Despite their limited influence, they are crucial to your project's success. You should actively consult with them and address their needs and feedback. These individuals are your allies, providing detailed insights and constructive feedback. They are an essential part of your communication strategy and should never be overlooked. You might find yourself having the most in-depth discussions with them, which can significantly support the successful launch of your project. It's important to keep them regularly updated and involved in the communication loop. Their engagement not only helps refine the project but also fosters a sense of ownership and satisfaction among them. Additionally, acknowledging their contributions and recognizing their role in the project's success is vital. This recognition can boost their morale and encourage continued support.

3. **Powerful Observers (Low Interest, High Influence),** at the bottom left of the matrix, are stakeholders who wield significant power but have limited interest in the project. They might include regulators, authorities, or competitors who can impact the project's environment or resources. It's crucial to monitor them and manage their expectations. I learned this the

hard way in one of my previous roles. Earlier in my career, I believed that as long as my boss and the primary project stakeholders were satisfied with the deliverables, we were successful. I was wrong. I reported to the head of HR at a global tech company and was tasked with rolling out a learning platform to facilitate digital learning for our thousands of global employees. My team and I focused on the technical aspects, collaborating with vendors, working with procurement, managing internal project leaders, and keeping my boss regularly updated. We launched on time and celebrated our success. However, during the project postmortem, my boss pointed out that we had failed to engage key influencers—individuals who, while not directly involved in the project, had strong opinions and wanted to be kept in the loop. This group included some of my peers and a leader from another team. I realized that my perception of stakeholders was incomplete. A four-quadrant exercise would have helped me identify where to focus my communication efforts. Since then, I have consistently used this exercise to ensure I don't overlook important influencers in my communication updates.

4. **Casual Bystanders (Low Interest, Low Influence),** at the bottom right of the matrix, are people who exhibit minimal interest in and influence over the project. Typically, this group encompasses the general public, media, or suppliers who are not directly involved or significantly affected by the project's outcomes. Although their engagement level is low, it is important to keep them informed and aware of the project's progress and key developments. For these stakeholders, a basic level of communication suffices, often categorized as FYI (For Your Information). Provide them with periodic updates, press releases, or newsletters to ensure they are aware of the project's existence and any major milestones. The goal is to

maintain transparency and foster a positive perception without overwhelming them with detailed information. By keeping casual bystanders in the loop, you can ensure that they remain informed and can act as passive supporters or neutral observers, contributing to a broader understanding and acceptance of the project within the community or industry.

When you start your new role with this exercise, guided by your new boss, you'll be able to identify the key people you need to connect with, both inside and outside your organization. Doing so will help you prioritize your tasks, a crucial skill during the often-overwhelming first few months of onboarding. The more senior your position, the greater the need for high-level prioritization to engage effectively with stakeholders and work on impactful projects for you, your team, and the organization. Keep in mind that these stakeholders will evolve as your journey within the organization progresses. They may also shift with each new project you undertake. Therefore, it's essential to keep this matrix at the forefront of your toolkit, using it to navigate your role and ensure continued success.

Now that you have gone through this exercise and identified several stakeholders in your new job, let's do a deeper dive into how to create a strong foundation with some of the most important stakeholders in your quadrants: your boss, your team, your customers, and your peers.

The Value of Adapting Your Communication Style

Anjali Sharma is a leading communication expert based in Singapore and is the founder and managing director of Narrative: The Business of Stories, a consultancy dedicated to helping organizations and individuals articulate and share their transformation stories. Additionally, she provides communication coaching to leaders to help them grow in their professional journeys.

I reached out to her for research on my book, to better understand different communication styles and their impact on building relationships within organizations. Anjali shared an insightful example; she spoke about a client who had achieved significant success in a mid-size company with a fast-paced culture. This client, let's call her Tony, had developed a reputation as a straight shooter, directly approaching decision makers and refusing to take no for an answer. On paper, Tony appeared to be the perfect go getter. However, when Tony transitioned to a new role in a well-established company with a large global brand and a different culture, she faced unexpected challenges.

Despite Anjali's advice to carefully unfold her story and experience in the new organization, Tony decided to dive in headfirst, confident in her abilities. A few months later, Tony reached out to Anjali; she was struggling to build relationships and accomplish her goals. Through coaching sessions, Anjali helped Tony identify the necessary changes to adapt her communication style to the new culture. Tony reflected on her observations and developed strategies for better communication with her team, peers, and boss. Anjali's key advice for anyone who takes on a new role in a new organization is not to focus on oneself and one's achievements but rather be there to say "How can I help you?" or "How can I help to move the business forward?"

After implementing these strategies, Tony began to see positive results, successfully integrating into the new organization and achieving her objectives. This experience underscores the importance of adapting communication styles to fit different organizational cultures and the value of thoughtful preparation and coaching.

Your Boss: The Most Important Person

It is hoped that, during the interview process, you met your new manager. Since they're the most important person to build a relationship with, I recommend giving them your highest priority.

Do additional research on your boss before you start your job. Read their LinkedIn profile to get to know them better. Having that information in your mind helps you to break the ice after you come on board.

Managing Your Boss

In my published dissertation (Miglani, 2021), I interviewed several new hires in an organization to ask about their experience when they joined their new role. One of the questions that I asked in my interview process was: Who helped them to assimilate in their new team? The ones who had a positive experience during their first 30 to 60 days were the ones whose managers spent time with them and helped them to create a plan to meet their team and cross-functional leaders. They also said that their managers helped them to understand the team dynamics and the company culture better. Twenty-six percent of the participants in this research had a bad experience with their managers, and several of them were ready to jump ship and find other roles.

Good bosses will set benchmarks and expectations for new hires, and they will help you to interpret your actions as a new team member for other key players and stakeholders in your company.

To build trust with your manager for a positive work environment and career growth, follow the next steps.

- **Review your job description together.** Schedule regular check-ins with your manager to discuss your role and responsibilities. Doing so ensures you're both aligned on what needs to be done.
- **Make concrete goals.** Instead of setting a vague goal, such as "Improve sales," set a specific target, such as "Make 20 sales calls per week."

- **Explore solutions before asking for help.** If you encounter a problem, think of possible solutions first. For instance, if a project is delayed, consider ways to expedite the process before consulting your manager.

- **Be transparent and agreeable if you make a mistake.** If you miss a deadline, inform your manager immediately and explain how you plan to avoid similar issues in the future.

- **Follow through on promises.** If you commit to completing a report by Friday, ensure it's done on time. Doing this builds reliability and trust.

- **Communicate clearly and often.** Regularly update your team on your progress and any challenges you're facing. Doing so keeps everyone informed and aligned.

Trust is built over time through consistent actions and genuine interactions. By following these steps, you can strengthen your relationship with your manager and grow in your career.

During my time at a software company, I hired an experienced senior manager to oversee key aspects of technology and operations. On her first day, she arrived prepared with questions. As her hiring manager, I made sure to equip her with comprehensive information about processes, teams, projects, and our top three objectives for the fiscal year. Confident that I had provided everything she needed, I believed I had fulfilled my responsibility.

However, right before our first one-on-one meeting, she introduced me to a new approach. She sent me an email listing the questions she wanted to discuss. Although I found this unusual, I decided to go along with it. This experience taught me that receiving questions in advance allowed me to prepare more effectively. As her inquiries became more technical, I could research answers beforehand, ensuring productive discussions during our meetings. Her goal was to maximize our time together, and I supported her in doing so. While I had conducted many similar meetings before, typically relying on my own notes, I realized I had never given my employees the opportunity to come prepared themselves.

Sharing Progress with Your Boss

Part of trust building is making sure your boss can have your back to support you and to remove roadblocks from your path. Bosses can do this only if you are diligent in sharing your progress with them. Sharing incremental progress updates with your boss is vital for multiple reasons. First, it fosters trust and transparency. Keeping your boss informed about your progress demonstrates your reliability and commitment, leading to stronger working relationships and improved communication. Second, regular updates enhance decision making. By providing progress reports, you equip your boss with essential information to make informed decisions about resource allocation, project timelines, and necessary adjustments. Third, progress reports help you manage expectations. Bosses who are aware of your ongoing work and progress can set realistic expectations and avoid surprises, which reduces stress and boosts overall productivity.

Research backs the importance of incremental progress updates. A study by Teresa Amabile and Steven Kramer, published under the title "The Power of Small Wins" in the *Harvard Business Review* (2011), highlights that making progress in meaningful work is a critical driver of positive inner work life, influencing emotions, motivations, and perceptions crucial to performance. They emphasize that small wins and incremental progress can significantly enhance motivation and creativity.

Providing incremental progress updates builds trust, improves decision making, manages expectations, and boosts motivation and creativity. It's a straightforward yet powerful method to enhance work performance and strengthen professional relationships.

Managing Meetings with Your Boss

Here's an eight-step template to follow for one-on-one meetings with your boss. Remember to adapt it to your specific needs and preferences.

1. **Check-ins and personal updates.** Depending on your company and geographical culture, this icebreaker can be personal or more professional. For instance, people often ask "How was your weekend?" as an icebreaker. Doing so usually helps to start meetings off on the right foot.

2. **Wins and achievements.** Discuss recent accomplishments or positive outcomes. Celebrate wins, both big and small.

3. **Challenges and roadblocks.** Highlight any obstacles you're facing. Share what you have tried or solutions you're considering. Seek advice or input from your boss.

4. **Progress on goals.** Review progress on your goals and projects. Share updates, milestones, and any adjustments needed.

5. **Feedback and development.** Request feedback on your performance. Discuss areas for improvement and growth. Explore development opportunities.

6. **Team progress.** If you are a team leader, use this opportunity to provide updates on how your team is doing, especially if you have someone who needs to be acknowledged for their work. Also highlight any performance issues with a team member during your one-to-one sessions.

7. **Action items and next steps.** Summarize key takeaways from the meeting. Agree on action items and deadlines.

8. **Closing remarks.** Confirm the date and time for the next meeting.

Meetings with your boss are valuable opportunities to build a strong working relationship, seek guidance, and align your goals with the organization's objectives.

Other Ways to Build Trust with Your Boss

You now have the information to create useful and trust-building meetings with your boss. What should you be doing on a daily basis? Stephen Covey and Rebecca Merrill, in their book *The Speed of Trust* (2006), outline several principles and strategies for building trust in professional relationships. To build trust with your new boss, you can apply Covey and Merrill's principles:

- **Show integrity.** Integrity is the foundation of trust. Be honest, transparent, and reliable in your interactions with your new boss. Keep your commitments, follow through on your promises, and act with integrity in all situations.

- **Demonstrate competence.** Competence builds credibility and trust. Strive to excel in your role, demonstrate expertise, and consistently deliver high-quality work. Take initiative to learn new skills, seek feedback for improvement, and demonstrate a willingness to grow and develop professionally. Manu Mehta, CEO of Cogent Infotech, a successful mid-size tech company, shares that new employees are expected to be proactive and ready to wear many different hats in the company. Unlike large companies, where processes are already in place, smaller companies and startups are ramping up on their products and processes. When they hire new employees, they want this individual to learn fast, jump in with both feet, and raise their hand to do more.

- **Clarify expectations.** Seek clarity on your boss's expectations for your role, responsibilities, and performance. Have open and honest conversations to ensure alignment and understanding. Proactively communicate your goals, priorities, and progress, and seek feedback to ensure you're meeting expectations.

- **Communicate openly and transparently.** Foster open communication with your boss by sharing information, insights, and feedback openly and transparently. Be approachable, listen actively, and encourage your boss to do the same. Create a safe space for honest dialogue where concerns can be addressed constructively.

- **Seek to understand.** Practice empathetic listening, and seek to understand your boss's perspective, priorities, and concerns. Show genuine interest in the boss's goals, challenges, and aspirations. Ask thoughtful questions, acknowledge their perspective, and demonstrate empathy and respect in your interactions.

- **Collaborate and support.** Build trust by collaborating effectively with your boss and supporting their goals and objectives. Be a team player, contribute ideas and insights, and offer your assistance when needed. Demonstrate a willingness to go above and beyond to help your boss succeed.

- **Admit mistakes and learn from them.** No one is perfect. When you make a mistake, take ownership of it, apologize if necessary, and learn from the experience. Show humility, resilience, and a commitment to continuous improvement. Use setbacks as opportunities to demonstrate your integrity and growth mindset.

- **Be consistent.** Be consistent in your actions, behaviors, and communication. Demonstrate reliability, predictability, and dependability in your work and interactions with your boss.

By applying these principles and strategies, you can build trust with your new boss and establish a strong foundation for a productive and positive working relationship. Trust takes time to develop, so be patient, consistent, and proactive in building trusting relationships. To understand what leaders seek when hiring and their expectations for new hires to integrate into the company culture, I interviewed Brandon Sammut, chief people officer at Zapier. In this role, he oversees people operations, culture, and talent strategies. Zapier, a leading automation platform for web applications, is renowned for its innovative onboarding practices.

I asked Brandon for advice on how new hires can quickly grasp the company culture and accelerate their learning. He replied, "Building trust and rapport is the foundation for any positive impact in a new job." To facilitate this, Zapier encourages new hires to create a "Read Me" document—a two-page guide about themselves, including their values, work style, and preferred feedback methods. This document is intended to be shared with the new manager, team, and key peers to facilitate seamless collaboration.

This practice systematically builds trust and rapport. Brandon also advised: "Approach your first period in a new role with humility. Be open about what you don't know and ask for help when needed. This builds a strong foundation of trust."

Building Trust with Direct Reports

If you are in a leadership role, understanding the people in your team should be one of your top priorities. The team's success is your success. If you are in a completely new role in the company, you get the chance to create your team by designing it and hiring the right people. In my career, I usually inherit existing teams. In one job, I spent the first 30 days doing meet-and-greet sessions with my team. These sessions helped me get to know each person on a personal level. However, within my first few sessions, I realized I was so lost in the personal talk that I didn't achieve my goal of learning about each of them on a *professional* level along with the key projects they were working on. Through trial and error, I figured out a meeting structure that worked well to access the information I needed.

Communication as a Leader

No matter what job you are in, communication is an important skill to have. It is even more important if you are a leader. How can you use this strength when you are new to a situation and expected to move projects along in your new role? Anneka Gupta, the chief product officer at Rubrik, a leading global cloud data management company based in Palo Alto, California, proves my point about communication.

Anneka joined Rubrik in July 2021 when the offices were still closed due to the pandemic. Her onboarding was entirely remote for the first six months. She recognized the challenge of entering a new industry and working with a team she didn't know well. Anneka emphasized the importance of gaining her team's trust and building cross-functional relationships. She arranged one-on-one meetings with her direct reports in person and outdoors before officially starting. Doing so helped her understand them better in an informal setting. Although she didn't have a strict 90-day plan, Anneka focused on adapting to the situation and learning as she went. She identified areas where she could add value, such as improving the effectiveness of product strategy meetings by helping product managers communicate their points more compellingly. Anneka's approach included being intentional about learning and adapting her strategies based on the company's needs and her observations. She helped her team craft their presentations, which allowed her to learn more about the product and the business.

While Anneka dedicated several weeks and months to focusing on her team, I've observed some leaders who spend this crucial time overselling themselves and their past experiences, thereby missing the opportunity to establish a strong foundation with their team from the outset. As a leader stepping into a new role, meeting your team in person is vital to:

- **Establish trust and rapport.** Face-to-face interactions allow you to build trust and rapport with your team members. Meeting in person creates a more personal connection, making it easier for team members to approach you, share their concerns, and collaborate effectively.

- **Understand team dynamics.** Observing team dynamics firsthand helps you understand how individuals interact, their communication styles, and any existing challenges. This insight enables you to tailor your leadership approach and address any underlying issues.

- **Set expectations.** In-person meetings provide an opportunity to clearly communicate your expectations, goals, and vision for the team. They allow you to align everyone's understanding and create a shared sense of purpose.

- **Assess individual strengths and weaknesses.** Meeting team members allows you to assess their strengths, weaknesses, and unique abilities. This knowledge helps you assign tasks appropriately and leverage each person's skills effectively.

- **Recognize nonverbal cues.** Nonverbal cues, such as body language and facial expressions, convey valuable information. By meeting in person, you can pick up on these cues, which may not be evident during virtual interactions.

- **Build team cohesion.** Face-to-face interactions foster team cohesion. Team-building activities, casual conversations, and shared experiences contribute to a positive team culture.

- **Navigate challenges.** When challenges arise, meeting in person allows for open discussions and problem solving. It's easier to address conflicts, clarify misunderstandings, and find solutions when you're physically present.

- **Demonstrate commitment.** Taking the time to meet your team demonstrates your commitment to their success while showing that you value their contributions and are invested in their growth.

Consider the next points when setting up an introductory meeting with your team members.

- **The invite.** Every company has different rules for meeting lengths. If you have a large team, you might need more time to get introductions going and to support an engaging Q&A at the end. I recommend 60 minutes for an initial meeting with them. Also ask your hiring manager about any meeting rules in your organization. In one of my previous companies, we had a written rule that meetings would start 5 minutes after the hour. This gave people time to take a breather between meetings, and it was widely adopted in our company.

- **Time zone.** When I worked at Micron, I had team members in six different time zones. Hosting a team meeting with people across time zones is challenging and requires a lot of support and planning from my team. For your initial introductory meeting, learn what time slots work best for them. For another large team I managed, I had two different sessions to accommodate those living in various time zones. The meeting day was long for me, but I was able to cover everyone in the group within 24 hours.

- **Agenda in the invitation.** A pet peeve of mine is when no agenda items are listed in the meeting invitation. State your goals in the invite. Creating an agenda is a great way to show respect for the time that you are asking of others and to show that you are coming prepared. It also gives others an opportunity to come prepared to show any updates or documentation and to invite any other team member or peer who might be a good addition to cover the agenda topics.

These tips are good for any type of meeting you are planning to have, whether it is with peers, your team, or your boss. They are the foundation of good meeting ethics.

When setting up an introductory meeting with your team, it's crucial to create a positive and engaging experience.

Seven Tips for Hosting an Effective Introductory Meeting

1. **Set a Clear Purpose**

    - **Define the purpose** of the meeting. Is it to welcome new team members, build relationships, or share your leadership philosophy?

    - **Craft a concise agenda** that outlines the meeting's objectives.

2. **Share a Collaborative Agenda**

    - **Distribute the agenda** in advance to all participants. Include topics, time allocations, and any relevant materials.

    - **Encourage input.** Allow team members to add agenda items or suggest discussion points.

3. **Invite Only Relevant Participants**

   - **Invite team members directly involved** in the introduction process.

   - **Avoid overloading the meeting.** Keep it focused and efficient.

4. **Begin by Introducing Yourself**

   - **Briefly share your background.** Highlight your professional journey and key experiences.

   - **Express your enthusiasm.** Show genuine interest in getting to know your team.

5. **Provide an Opportunity for Questions**

   - **Allocate time for Q&A.** Let team members ask about your role, expectations, or anything else.

   - **Be approachable and open.** Foster a comfortable environment for dialogue.

6. **Establish Expectations**

   - **Clarify team norms.** Discuss communication channels, meeting frequency, and collaboration tools.

   - **Set the tone for collaboration.** Emphasize openness, respect, and teamwork.

7. **Assign Clear Next Steps**

   - **Summarize action items.** Ensure everyone knows what to do after the meeting.

   - **Follow up.** Send thank-you emails and any relevant resources discussed during the meeting.

Setting Up Regular Town Halls

Quarterly town hall meetings for your team are essential for communication, alignment, and transparency. You don't have to use all the topics discussed next. Depending on how much time you have for these sessions and what you want to achieve, you can include the key components listed next.

Quarterly Town Hall Meeting Agenda

1. **Welcome and Introduction**
   - Greet everyone and set a positive tone.
   - Briefly introduce yourself (if needed).

2. **Review of Previous Quarter's Goals and Achievements**
   - Recap the goals set in the last town hall.
   - Highlight achievements, milestones, and challenges overcome.

3. **Financial Update**
   - Present financial performance (revenue, expenses, profits).
   - Discuss any budget adjustments or financial priorities.

4. **Team Updates and Announcements**
   - Each team lead shares updates specific to their area.
   - Announce new hires, promotions, or departures.
   - Highlight team wins and recognize outstanding contributions.

5. **Strategic Initiatives and Roadmap**
   - Discuss upcoming projects, product launches, or strategic shifts.
   - Share the company's vision and long-term goals.

6. Q&A Session

- Open the floor for questions from team members.
- Address concerns, clarify doubts, and encourage participation.

7. Employee Spotlight

- Feature an outstanding employee or team.
- Share their achievements and contributions.

8. Recognition and Appreciation

- Acknowledge exceptional work.
- Express gratitude to the entire team.

9. Upcoming Events and Reminders

- Highlight any company-wide events, workshops, or training sessions.
- Remind everyone of important dates.

10. Closing Remarks

- Summarize key takeaways.
- Encourage collaboration and teamwork.

    Adapt this format to your team's specific needs and culture.

Developing Positive Relationships with Your Peers

During the interview process for your new role, I hope you had a chance to meet your new boss and additional senior leaders. In some cases, you might also have met a some team members and stakeholders. However, it's not common to meet your peers before you start a new job. Here are some tips to help you make a good first impression and start building positive relationships with your coworkers.

Be Punctual and Consistent

Arriving on time and being prepared for the day's tasks are fundamental practices that can significantly impact how both your employer and your colleagues view your professionalism. Although it may seem obvious, punctuality and preparedness are clear demonstrations of your dependability and responsibility.

Consider the case of a senior manager who was highly regarded and brought a wealth of experience to his role as a product manager. His insights during meetings were invaluable, and his engagement with the team was notable. However, when a promotion opportunity arose, he was overlooked. The primary reason? His habitual tardiness to meetings, last-minute cancellations, and delays in responding to emails and inquiries. These behaviors projected an image of unpredictability and unreliability, overshadowing his otherwise commendable performance. Once he received feedback and understood the importance of being punctual and consistent, he made significant progress and was promoted a year later.

Cultivate Friendliness and Exude Confidence

A warm smile and steady eye contact can set the stage for positive interactions with your new colleagues. Take the initiative to introduce yourself, offering a glimpse into your professional journey and the role you've assumed. Express your eagerness to collaborate and learn alongside your team. This blend of a positive outlook and self-assured presence is instrumental in forging lasting impressions. My good friend Ryan Weber, the Chief Talent Officer at BetterUp, advocates for establishing personal connections before delving into work-related discussions. Upon

> A warm smile and steady eye contact can set the stage for positive interactions with your new colleagues.

entering a new position, especially one where you inherit a team or step into a predecessor's shoes, your peers may feel uncertain about the impending changes. By prioritizing the human element—getting to know your colleagues on a personal level—you can alleviate their anxieties. This approach encourages openness, fostering an environment where walls come down, paving the way for genuine connections.

Listen to Learn

As a new hire, one of the most valuable skills you can cultivate is the ability to listen with the intent to learn, rather than simply preparing to reply. This approach demonstrates respect and value for the perspectives of others. For example, consider a scenario where a new employee, June, joins a team that is in the midst of a complex project. During meetings, June makes a conscious effort to listen attentively to the discussions, asks clarifying questions, and takes notes. Instead of jumping in with immediate solutions or opinions, June focuses on understanding the nuances of the project and the team's dynamics. After a few weeks, June uses the insights gained from listening to propose a solution that addresses a long-standing challenge the team has been facing. This proposal highlights June's problem-solving skills and reflects a deep understanding of the team's work, earning her the respect and trust of colleagues. By listening to learn, June was able to integrate effectively into the team and make a meaningful contribution early on.

This story illustrates the power of active listening in fostering learning, collaboration, and professional growth.

As a new hire, one of the most valuable skills you can cultivate is the ability to listen with the intent to learn, rather than simply preparing to reply.

Be Willing to Help

Embrace the opportunity to inquire and request assistance as necessary; doing so demonstrates to your colleagues your commitment to learning and self-improvement. Similarly, be ready to extend a helping hand. Proactively engaging in projects or assignments is an effective way to highlight your capabilities and contribute value. In *Lean In: Women, Work, and the Will to Lead*, Sheryl Sandberg highlights the significance of taking on extra responsibilities and projects to propel your career forward. She advocates for "leaning in" by volunteering for challenging tasks and stepping outside your comfort zone. According to Sandberg, this approach not only showcases your abilities but also helps you gain valuable experience and increase your visibility within the organization. She cautions against letting fear of failure or self-doubt hold you back, encouraging readers to seize opportunities that push their skills and foster professional growth. This proactive mindset can lead to enhanced career development and open up leadership opportunities.

Be Approachable

Make an effort to connect with your colleagues beyond work-related matters. Learn their names and take an interest in their lives outside of the office, whether it's their passion for gardening, their weekend hiking adventures, or their family milestones. When the moment is right, engage in lighthearted conversations and participate in company gatherings and team-building activities. Such interactions can foster a sense of camaraderie and establish a foundation of trust among team members. Let's say your new company has a variety of employee interest groups, such as a book club, a coding guild, and a fitness squad. You decide to join the book club, where you meet fellow enthusiasts who gather monthly to discuss the latest read.

During these sessions, you not only share insights on the book but also learn about each member's favorite genres, authors, and literary experiences. This shared passion for reading becomes a common ground for deeper conversations and connections.

Tips to Build Trust with Peers

- **Be self-aware.** Recognize your communication strengths and areas for growth. For instance, if you tend to avoid conflict, practice having difficult conversations with a mentor to improve your conflict resolution skills.

- **Be dependable.** Consistently meet deadlines and maintain transparency with your peers if you are working on cross-functional projects with them. If you commit to delivering a project by Friday, ensure it's ready or, if there's a delay, communicate it promptly and honestly.

- **Embrace team diversity.** Understand and value the unique roles and viewpoints of your colleagues. Take time to learn about the challenges coworkers face, fostering mutual respect and appreciation.

- **Be a team player.** Actively collaborate and share the limelight. During group projects, openly exchange ideas and acknowledge each member's contributions, such as giving a shout-out to the designer for creative input during a team meeting.

- **Be an open communicator.** Build relationships by initiating conversations that go beyond work. Show genuine interest in your colleagues' lives. For example, if a coworker enjoys photography, ask about their favorite subjects to photograph.

- **Offer support proactively.** Help others before they ask, whether it's assisting a new team member with company software or volunteering for an urgent task.

The stories I've shared about Tom Brady, Jacinda Ardern, and more illustrate the qualities and abilities needed for you to succeed in your new role. When you combine preparation and the willingness to learn efficiently with developing goals, you'll be well on your way to career success. Strategy #2 focuses on how building the right goals will help you.

Career Pointers

1. Identify and list your key stakeholders.

2. Classify these key stakeholders according to the matrix.

3. If your boss agrees, set up a regular time to meet with them.

4. Take steps to build trust with your boss, direct reports, and other colleagues.

5. If needed, review the steps to set up effective town hall meetings.

Goal Setting and Feedback

Setting goals is the first step in turning the invisible into visible.

—Tony Robbins

THE CONCEPT OF GOAL SETTING has deep roots in human history, but its systematic application in the context of the industrial age can be traced back to the late 19th and early 20th centuries. The Industrial Revolution fundamentally transformed work, organization, and management, paving the way for innovative strategies to enhance productivity and performance.

One of the earliest proponents of goal setting in the industrial age was Frederick Winslow Taylor, often regarded as the father of scientific management. Taylor's work, particularly his book *The Principles of Scientific Management*, first published in 1911 (2012), emphasized the importance of setting clear and specific goals for workers in order to achieve maximum efficiency and productivity. Taylor believed that breaking tasks down into smaller, more manageable components and setting quantifiable performance targets would motivate workers to exert greater effort and achieve higher levels of output.

Taylor's ideas laid the foundation for the development of goal-setting theory, which gained further prominence in the mid-20th century. One of the key figures in this field was Peter Drucker, a management consultant and author whose writings on management theory had a profound influence on organizational practices.

In his seminal work, *The Practice of Management* (2006), Drucker emphasized the importance of setting objectives as a fundamental management function. He introduced the concept of Management by Objectives (MBO), which involved setting specific, measurable, achievable, relevant, and time-bound (SMART) goals that aligned with organizational objectives. Drucker argued that managers could enhance motivation, clarity of purpose, and accountability by involving employees in the goal-setting process and providing them with feedback on their performance.

The application of goal-setting principles expanded rapidly in the latter half of the 20th century, fueled by advancements in management theory and technology. Organizations across industries adopted goal-setting frameworks such as MBO and cascading goals to align individual and team objectives with broader organizational goals. The concept of key performance indicators (KPIs) gained traction as a means of measuring progress toward goals and evaluating performance.

Goal setting became a cornerstone of performance management systems in the industrial age, providing a structured approach to planning, execution, and evaluation. However, critics have highlighted potential drawbacks, such as the risk of goal displacement, where employees prioritize achieving targets at the expense of broader organizational goals, and the potential for demotivation if goals are perceived as unrealistic or unattainable.

Why Do Goals Matter?

Goal setting and feedback are crucial components of professional development and success in any job, but they are particularly important in a new job for several reasons.

- **Clarity and direction.** Setting clear, achievable goals helps you understand what is expected of you in your new role and allows you to prioritize tasks and allocate your time and resources effectively.

- **Motivation and engagement.** Having goals to work toward can boost motivation and engagement in your new job. When you have a clear sense of purpose and direction, you are more likely to feel invested in your work and committed to achieving success.

- **Accountability.** Setting goals creates accountability and allows you to track your progress and performance, ensuring that you stay on track and take responsibility for your actions and outcomes.

- **Continuous improvement.** Feedback plays a critical role in identifying areas for improvement and growth. Constructive feedback from supervisors, colleagues, and mentors helps you understand your strengths and weaknesses, enabling you to develop new skills and enhance your performance over time.

- **Alignment with organizational objectives.** Goal setting ensures that your individual goals are aligned with the broader objectives of the organization and helps you understand how your work contributes to the overall mission and vision, fostering a sense of purpose and alignment with organizational priorities.

- **Professional development.** Regular feedback provides valuable insights into your performance and areas for development while enabling you to identify learning opportunities, seek out relevant training or mentorship, and continuously improve your skills and capabilities.

Overall, goal setting and feedback are essential tools for navigating the challenges of a new job, clarifying expectations, staying motivated, and driving professional growth and success. They facilitate communication, alignment, and continuous improvement, helping you thrive in your new role and make meaningful contributions to your organization.

Steve Jobs: A Leader in Goal Setting

One leader often cited as one of the best for goal setting is Steve Jobs, the cofounder of Apple Inc. Jobs was renowned for his visionary leadership style and his ability to set ambitious yet achievable goals that inspired and motivated his team to extraordinary feats of innovation and creativity.

Jobs was a firm believer in the power of setting audacious goals that pushed the boundaries of what seemed possible. He famously challenged his team to "put a dent in the universe," encouraging them to think big and pursue groundbreaking ideas. Jobs set clear and compelling objectives for Apple, such as revolutionizing personal computing with products like the Macintosh, transforming the music industry with the iPod and iTunes, and reinventing the smartphone with the iPhone. Jobs's goal-setting prowess was evident in his relentless pursuit of excellence and his unwavering commitment to delivering products that delighted customers.

Jobs was adept at aligning his team around common goals and inspiring them to perform at their best. He was known for his charismatic leadership style, his ability to communicate a compelling vision, and his knack for rallying people around a shared purpose. By instilling a sense of passion and purpose in his team, Jobs fostered a culture of innovation and collaboration that propelled Apple to unprecedented success.

How Performance Management Works with Goals

Performance management is a strategic and systematic process that aims to improve employee performance by setting clear expectations, providing ongoing feedback, and offering development opportunities. W. D. Scott is credited with inventing performance appraisals during World War I. However, his system wasn't widely recognized. Not until the mid-20th century did more formal appraisal systems gain traction in businesses. By the mid-1950s, formal performance appraisals were common. These systems often used personality-based approaches, but they lacked self-appraisal and effective performance monitoring. Over the next two decades, companies emphasized employee motivation and engagement.

New metrics like self-awareness, communication, teamwork, conflict reduction, and emotional handling became part of performance reviews.

Highlights of Performance Management:

Next we focus on the purpose and definition of performance management.

- **Purpose.** Performance management helps individuals perform to the best of their abilities while aligning their efforts with the organization's overall goals.

- **Definition.** Performance management is a tool used by managers to monitor and evaluate employees' work, fostering an environment of accountability and transparency.

Consider the next core elements of performance management:

- **Contextual view.** Performance management considers individuals within the broader workplace system, recognizing their impact on organizational success.

- **Goal setting.** Employees actively participate in defining goals, ensuring alignment with company objectives. Later in this chapter, we discuss the different ways of setting your goals and working with your leader/manager on constantly seeking feedback.

- **Ongoing feedback.** Unlike annual reviews, performance management provides continuous feedback to employees.

- **Measurement and adjustment.** Traditional tools like goal setting and milestones are used, but every interaction becomes a learning opportunity.

Performance management works via:

- **Alignment.** Managers and employees collaborate to set expectations, define goals, and understand career progress.

- **Budget allocation.** Performance management guides the allocation of funds within the company's performance budget.

- **Feedback loop.** Managers adjust workflows, recommend actions, and make decisions to help employees achieve their objectives.

The benefits of performance management include:

- **Healthier environment.** Focusing on continuous accountability creates transparency and reduces workplace stress.

- **Clear expectations.** Everyone understands what's expected, leading to better performance.

- **Improved communication.** Regular meetings enhance overall communication.

Goal Setting and Types of Goal Setting in Organizations

Effective goal setting is essential for personal and professional growth. The best way to learn about the way your organization manages goals is to work directly with your manager to understand the process. Let's explore five popular goal-setting models and frameworks that can help you achieve your objectives.

1. **Objectives and key results (OKRs)** form a powerful goal-setting framework used by individuals, teams, and organizations to define measurable goals and track their outcomes. Objectives are ambitious, qualitative goals that provide direction and purpose, while key results are specific, measurable outcomes that indicate progress toward achieving these objectives. Developed by Andrew Grove at Intel in the 1970s, OKRs gained popularity as a way to align teams and drive performance. Unlike traditional top-down approaches, OKRs involve a collaborative process where teams refine high-level objectives for specific areas, ensuring alignment with overall organizational goals. This approach increases engagement as team members understand the significance of their tasks. The benefits of OKRs include providing a clear roadmap for what needs to be achieved, allowing for progress tracking through key results, and increasing SMART goals.

2. **SMART goals (specific, measurable, achievable, relevant, and time-bound goals).** This framework ensures that goals are well-defined, realistic, and have a clear deadline. One example of a SMART goal is: "Increase website traffic by 20% within six months."

3. **Backward goals.** Start by envisioning your desired outcome and then work backward to identify the steps needed to achieve it. This method helps break down long-term goals into manageable tasks. For example, if your ultimate goal is to launch a successful startup, work backward to create milestones like building a prototype, securing funding, and launching the product.

4. **Think big, act small, move quickly (BSQ).** The BSQ method combines audacious thinking with practical action. Start with a big vision, break it down into smaller steps, and execute swiftly. For example, a startup aiming to revolutionize transportation might start by launching a pilot project in a specific city.

5. **Goal pyramid.** Imagine a pyramid with different layers representing your goals. The base layer consists of foundational goals (e.g., health, relationships), followed by intermediate goals (career, finances), and aspirational goals (dreams and passions). For example, the base layer could be to exercise regularly, the intermediate layer to achieve a promotion, and the aspirational layer to write a novel.

Key Performance Indicators

Key performance indicators (KPIs) can be used to create individual goals within a company. In fact, aligning individual goals with KPIs is a common practice that helps ensure employees' efforts are directly contributing to the organization's strategic objectives. Here's how KPIs can be used to create individual goals:

- **Identify relevant KPIs.** Begin by identifying the KPIs that are most relevant to the individual's role and responsibilities.

These should directly align with the contributor's departmental or organizational goals.

- **Set specific goals.** Based on the identified KPIs, set SMART goals for the individual. These goals should clearly outline the desired outcome or performance level related to each KPI.

- **Link goals to KPIs.** Clearly articulate how each individual goal is directly linked to one or more KPIs. Doing this helps employees understand the purpose and significance of their goals and how achieving them contributes to overall performance and success.

- **Establish performance targets.** Define performance targets or benchmarks for each individual goal, based on the desired level of performance indicated by the corresponding KPIs. Performance targets provide clear expectations and criteria for success.

- **Provide context and guidance.** Offer context and guidance to individuals on how they can achieve their goals and improve their performance in alignment with the identified KPIs. Doing this may involve providing training, resources, feedback, and support as needed.

- **Monitor progress and provide feedback.** Continuously monitor progress toward individual goals and KPIs, providing regular feedback and coaching to help employees stay on track and address any challenges or obstacles they may encounter.

By aligning individual goals with KPIs, organizations ensure that employees' efforts are focused on activities that directly impact organizational performance and success. This alignment also enhances accountability, transparency, and clarity around expectations, ultimately driving greater effectiveness and results at both the individual and organizational levels.

Setting effective goals at work is crucial for your professional success. Here are some strategies to help you set and achieve meaningful goals.

- **Understand your "why."** Connect every goal to a purpose. When you understand why you're pursuing a goal, it's easier to stay focused and avoid distractions.

- **Break goals down.** In 2018, Meng Zhu, an associate professor of marketing at the Johns Hopkins Carey Business School, published an insightful article in the *Harvard Business Review* titled "Why We Procrastinate When We Have Long Deadlines." The article delves into a study involving two groups of volunteers at a local community center. The volunteers were asked to complete a short survey about retirement planning. One group had a seven-day window to access the online survey, while the other had 14 days.

The findings of the study were quite revealing.

Participants with the 14-day deadline tended to spend more time on the task and wrote more extended responses compared to those with a seven-day deadline. This finding suggests that longer deadlines might lead to procrastination and overthinking, ultimately impacting productivity and efficiency. To counteract this tendency, it's beneficial to break down large goals into smaller, more manageable steps. By setting smaller, short-term goals, you can accomplish these tasks daily or weekly, which helps maintain momentum and ensures continuous progress. This approach can make the overall goal seem less daunting and more achievable, leading to increased productivity and a greater sense of accomplishment. For instance, if you're working on a large project at work, instead of setting a single, overwhelming deadline, you could break the project into smaller tasks. Create a timeline for each task, setting specific, shorter deadlines. This way, you'll be able to focus on one step at a time, track your progress more effectively, and reduce the urge to procrastinate. Moreover, celebrating small wins along the way can boost your motivation and keep you on track toward your ultimate goal.

In summary, setting smaller, time-bound goals can help mitigate procrastination, keep you focused, and lead to steady progress toward achieving your larger objectives.

- **Allocate buffer time.** Schedule extra time for your goals. Increase your estimated deadline by 25% to account for unexpected delays or challenges.

- **Focus on continuation.** Embrace what you've already started. Build on existing efforts rather than starting something new. Consistency matters.

- **Learn from past failures.** Understand that setbacks are normal. Everyone experiences ups and downs. Learn from failures and keep moving forward.

Remember, goal setting is an ongoing process. Regularly evaluate your progress, adjust as needed, and celebrate your achievements along the way.

The Importance of Feedback

Feedback is an essential tool for gaining insights and driving improvement. It acts like a mirror, reflecting our performance and helping us understand our strengths, areas for growth, and how others perceive us. "Performance feedback" is the practice of offering detailed insights into an individual's performance, with the goal of refining or sustaining their skill application. It falls under the broader umbrella of performance management, a concept introduced by Aubrey Daniels in the 1970s and continuously evolving since. Effective performance feedback plays a key role in boosting employee efficiency and strengthening organizational adaptability. In simpler terms, feedback highlights our strengths and areas for improvement, providing valuable insights for personal and professional development. In a tech company, feedback is crucial for continuous improvement and innovation. For example, software developers might receive feedback on their code quality, helping them refine their skills and produce more efficient code. Similarly, product managers might seek feedback from users to understand their needs better and improve the product's features. Seeking feedback is like adjusting a compass—it helps us stay on course and navigate toward improvement. By inviting others to share their observations and perspectives, we can continuously grow and enhance our performance.

In *Thanks for the Feedback: The Science and Art of Receiving Feedback Well*, Douglas Stone and Sheila Heen (2014) discuss the intricate world of feedback—why it's challenging to receive, how we react to it, and techniques to effectively discuss and integrate it into our lives.

Here's a concise overview of the book: Feedback is any information about ourselves, whether from experiences or other people, such as a test score, a compliment, or a formal appraisal. Despite the importance of feedback for learning, we often struggle to embrace feedback, especially the negative type. When giving feedback, we may feel the recipient isn't receiving it well. When receiving feedback, we may feel the giver isn't delivering it effectively. Our desire to learn often clashes with our desire for acceptance. Three triggers block feedback: truth triggers, which occur when we believe the feedback is wrong, unfair, or unhelpful; relationship triggers, which arise when we question the giver's authority to provide feedback; and identity triggers, which occur when feedback threatens our self-image. Feedback serves three distinct purposes: appreciation (motivation and encouragement), coaching (learning and growth), and evaluation (ranking or rating against a benchmark). Although many resources focus on giving better feedback, learning to receive feedback is equally crucial. Being adept at receiving feedback improves relationships, self-esteem, learning, and performance. Feedback is a mirror reflecting our growth.

I believe that asking for feedback demonstrates maturity, ownership, and autonomy while also increasing confidence and productivity. It fosters a culture where feedback is embraced, helping us understand how our work contributes to larger goals. Additionally, it encourages healthy dialogue, discussion, problem-solving, and innovation. To ask for feedback, start by reflecting on your goal and understanding what you hope to gain. Identify the right people who can provide relevant insights and prepare thoughtful questions related to your performance. Be open and receptive to create an environment where feedback is welcomed. After receiving feedback, follow up by considering how to apply it for growth.

For example, in the financial industry, financial analysts might seek feedback from their managers on their recent market analysis reports. Analysts could ask, "Can you provide specific feedback on my analysis of the recent market trends and suggest areas for improvement?" This approach not only helps analysts improve their skills but also aligns their work with the company's strategic goals. When asking for feedback via email, let the recipient know you're seeking to improve, be direct about the specific help you're asking for, and make it easy for them to respond. For instance, an email might say: "I'm looking to improve my market analysis reports. Could you please review my latest report and provide feedback on areas where I can enhance my analysis and presentation?" This clear and direct approach facilitates constructive feedback and supports professional growth.

STAR: A "Feedback" Model

Having spent two decades in HR and learning, I've collaborated with many leaders with diverse communication styles. Recently I reported to an industry veteran with nearly 30 years of experience. This man was deeply respected and invested significant time in nurturing his immediate team. However, despite his well-meaning intentions, he struggled with delivering feedback effectively. His feedback often felt detached, more like an impersonal observation than genuine insight, leaving his team confused and sometimes frustrated. Recognizing this challenge, I introduced him to the STAR model, a feedback model that had proven effective for me in the past. This model provided a clear structure, allowing him to focus his feedback and offer actionable advice. Once he grasped the concept, he found it much easier to have those conversations, thus continuing to foster the growth and development of his team.

The transformation was remarkable. His feedback became more impactful and his team responded positively, leading to a more cohesive and motivated group.

The STAR model, created by Development Dimensions International (DDI), offers a structured method for delivering feedback. The initialism "STAR" stands for *s*ituation, *t*ask, *a*ction, and *r*esult, which helps to provide clear, specific, and actionable feedback by breaking it down into four components:

1. **Situation.** Outline the context or specific situation that occurred.
2. **Task.** Define the task or challenge that needs to be addressed.
3. **Action.** Describe the actions taken to address the task.
4. **Result.** Share the outcome or result of those actions.

The STAR model can be a valuable tool for providing to and receiving feedback from company newcomers, ensuring a smooth transition and fostering a supportive work environment. Use it in this way:

Begin by describing a specific situation you encountered in your new role. For example: "During my first week, I observed that our team's project management process needed improvement."

Clearly state the task or challenge you identified. For instance: "I realized the need for a more structured approach to managing our projects efficiently."

Explain the actions you took to address the task. You might say, "I recommended the implementation of a project management tool and organized a training session to ensure everyone was on board."

Share the result of your actions. For example: "As a result, our project timelines improved, and the team's productivity increased by 20% within the first month."

Using the STAR model enables you to provide specific and actionable feedback, making it easier for new colleagues to understand your contributions and suggestions. It also allows you to receive structured feedback, helping you identify areas for improvement and grow in your new role.

Career Pointers

1. List your goals, and note why they matter to you.

2. Consider what *types* of goals your organization cares about the most.

3. Take time for reflection, so you can modify your actions and celebrate your wins.

Company Processes

"Do every job you're in like you're going to do it for the rest of your life, and demonstrate that ownership of it."
—Mart Barra, CEO of General Motors

WHEN I JOINED MY NEW company in San Francisco as head of talent enablement, my role included working on designing and launching company programs. These programs could range from new-hire onboarding and first-time manager training sessions to planning our performance management processes. Unfortunately, I figured out the hard way how to launch such programs. An unwritten process agreed on by the senior HR leaders was to get the review in front of the chief of people (CPO), get her approval, and prepare to launch. However, when I joined the company, the process was not part of my onboarding training or discussions. Just two days before our big launch, I met a fellow HR senior leader in the office kitchen as we were making our morning cups of coffee. The fellow leader casually asked me what was keeping me busy, and I told her how I was excited to launch this new program.

She replied, "Well, our chief people officer must have loved the concept to give you the green light for this."

My jaw dropped. I still remember the smell of the coffee and burning toast in the kitchen as I broke into a sweat. I asked her, "Is running the launch past the CPO part of the process?"

Once my colleague realized I had not been told about the process during my transition, she kindly sat me down and gave me examples of why this was part of the company process and what I could do to save the program. I immediately got on my CPO's calendar, got her approval, and shared how I had been this close to making a big mistake for my very first company program within my first 90 days. She laughed and then realized how she could have done better as my leader. From then on, when we hired anyone in her leadership group, we let them know about the approval process.

Once I learned about the process, I also was able to make changes to my working methods. The way I created timelines for my projects and planned the program launches had to change, but I discovered this a bit late, after I started the project. After I shared the presentation with my new CPO, I thought my message and timelines were ready to be communicated to my business leaders. I made the mistake of not asking my CPO about the next steps and just assumed that I could move forward once she gave me the thumbs up. She, in contrast, assumed that I knew the process of next presenting to senior leadership staff to get more approvals before it went to the CEO executive team for the final approval. We caught this mistake after my second round of discussions with a business/functional leader when she asked me if the CEO executive team had approved the project.

I reached out to my boss, the CPO, and that's when we both realized that we had made a few assumptions and should have talked about the approval process. I am lucky that my CPO was understanding, and we quickly made the change in our process. Overall, it's best to understand and ask and never assume how company processes function. These processes include those for project approvals, budget planning and approvals, requesting hardware and software apps, taking time off, and business travel.

Another type of approval or cultural norm that I have seen in companies and subteams concerns whether it is always necessary to ask for approvals or whether you can move fast to support the business and ask for forgiveness later. This topic is discussed in depth in Strategy #6: The Company Culture.

Learning the way things are done in your new organization is one of the key strategies you will need to focus on to be successful in your new role. This strategy entails leveraging your professional network, using online resources such as the company intranet and apps, and honing your powers of observation. Upon entering a new role, it is vital to cultivate the ability to observe. This observational skill must then transition into active learning, practical application, seeking feedback, adjusting course as necessary, all while maintaining a brisk pace of progress.

How You Benefit from Understanding Company Processes

Read on to learn how a deep understanding of the company's processes will help you.

- **Navigating efficiency** is essential for smooth sailing. Processes streamline operations, ensuring tasks are executed consistently and efficiently. If you don't understand these processes, you risk stumbling into inefficiencies or making avoidable mistakes, much like hitting potholes on an otherwise smooth road.

- **Alignment with the company's goals** is another critical aspect. Processes reflect the organization's DNA. By learning them, you align your efforts with the organization's mission and vision. When you grasp how each cog fits into the machine, you can contribute strategically, making a significant impact on the company's success.

- **Effective collaboration** is facilitated by well-understood processes. Think of it as team choreography; you'll know when to pass the baton and when to sprint ahead. Understanding these processes ensures everyone speaks the same language, which is essential for teamwork and achieving common goals.

- **Risk mitigation** is another vital reason to learn company processes. These processes often include risk management steps, and ignoring them could lead to costly detours. Compliance processes, in particular, keep you on the right side of legal and ethical boundaries, ensuring that your actions are aligned with company policies and regulations.

- **Adaptability and innovation** are also fostered by a deep understanding of processes. Processes evolve over time and, by learning them, you can identify areas ripe for improvement. Armed with this knowledge, you can propose innovative tweaks, turning your understanding into a playground for innovation.

This comprehensive understanding paves the way for you to focus on delivering your goals as you onboard, ensuring a smooth and successful integration into your new role.

Types of Company Processes

When starting at a new company, grasping key processes is crucial for a smooth transition and effective performance. Focus your energies on these main types of processes.

- **Onboarding process.** This process involves completing necessary paperwork, setting up your workstation, and gaining access to company systems. Since several of these processes may or may not be sequential in your organization, you can decide on the best way to read the chapters based on input you receive from your direct manager.

- **Communication channels.** It's essential to grasp how your company handles internal communication, which might involve emails, instant messaging apps like Slack or Microsoft Teams, and regular meetings. In Strategy #4: Technology, I explore various communication channels in detail. Once you identify which communication channels are used in your organization, you can use the information in Strategy #4 to make the most of them.

- **Performance management.** Familiarize yourself with how performance is evaluated. An example is understanding key performance indicators (KPIs), review cycles, and feedback mechanisms.

- **Company culture.** Pay attention to the company's values, norms, and behaviors, including how relationships are valued, how change is managed, and whether individual or group achievements are prioritized. For example, some companies have a strong team-oriented culture with regular team-building activities.

- **Decision-making processes.** Are the decisions top-down, collaborative, or consensus-driven? For instance, in some organizations, senior management might make major decisions, while in others, team discussions and votes play a significant role. Despite having been in the workforce for several years, I still had to adapt to new decision-making methods in one of my new jobs. It is important to be flexible and open to learning different approaches to managing tasks and responsibilities.

- **HR policies.** Get to know the human resources policies, including leave policies, benefits, and any compliance-related procedures. For example, it is essential to understand the process for requesting vacation time or the details of your health insurance plan.

- **IT and security protocols.** Learn about the IT support process, data security measures, and any specific software or tools you need to use. For example, you might need to follow specific guidelines for password management and data encryption.

- **Project management.** Understand the project management methodologies and tools used, such as Agile, Scrum, or traditional project management techniques. If the company uses Agile, for example, you might participate in sprint planning and daily stand-ups.

Some suggestions on the best way to get started are listed next.

- **Your manager is the key.** As part of your ongoing discussion with your direct manager, make sure to discuss and clarify the usual project approval process. Having a verbal agreement with your manager will also help to have your back if things don't go as planned. When in doubt, ask.

- **Access HR resources.** In many states, it's legally required to provide access to HR resources digitally and to have it posted in office areas. I've noticed that several companies choose to display these policies in common areas like break rooms or printer rooms, or around the water cooler. If you're ever in doubt, you can reach out to the HR recruiter you initially worked with, your team's business partner, or, as mentioned earlier, your reporting manager.

- **Continue to observe.** When you are part of a team, you also get a chance to be part of project updates and presentations by your peers and cross-functional team members. As they present and follow different steps to make their project successful, you will learn several key tips on what works in your new company.

Pay Attention to HR Policies to Help You Achieve Your Goals

These points aim to highlight a few key areas you should focus on to avoid confusion and ensure a smooth onboarding process. By paying attention to these points, you can concentrate on achieving your goals more effectively as you settle into your new office culture.

Office Hours and Attendance Policies

These policies establish the expected working hours, designated break times, and attendance requirements for employees. They often include specific guidelines for reporting absences or tardiness, ensuring that everyone is aware of the procedures to follow in case they cannot make it to work on time or need to take a day off. Adhering to these policies is crucial for maintaining a smooth workflow and ensuring that all team members can rely on each other. Following the established office hours and attendance guidelines helps prevent disruptions in the workflow and ensures that deadlines are met. This reliability is essential for fostering a productive and cohesive work environment.

For example, if your company has a policy that requires employees to be at their desks by 9:00 am, consistently arriving late can cause delays in team meetings, project timelines, and overall productivity. Similarly, if specific break times are outlined, taking breaks outside of these times can disrupt the flow of work and affect team coordination. Moreover, failing to adhere to attendance policies can lead to a perception of unreliability among your colleagues and supervisors, which can impact your professional reputation and may result in disciplinary actions, such as warnings or even termination in severe cases. Communicate any absences or tardiness promptly and follow the proper reporting procedures to maintain transparency and trust within your team. Consistently following office hours and attendance policies demonstrates your commitment to your role and respect for your colleagues' time. It shows that you are dependable and take your responsibilities seriously, which can positively influence your career progression and opportunities for advancement.

Remote Work Policies

Understanding and adhering to remote work policies is a fundamental aspect of integrating smoothly into your new role. Such adherence helps you build a strong foundation of reliability and professionalism, which are key to long-term success in any organization. Remote work policies set clear expectations and guidelines for employees working from home or other remote locations. These policies typically cover various aspects, such as work hours, availability, communication protocols, and data security measures. Adhering to these policies is crucial to avoid misunderstandings about your availability, to maintain productivity, and to prevent potential security breaches. The importance of remote work policies has increased significantly, especially in the post-COVID era. The pandemic made remote work a necessity, prompting both employees and employers to adjust their working arrangements to ensure safety. Although remote work offered flexibility and safety during the pandemic, many organizations faced challenges when transitioning back to traditional office schedules.

To address these challenges, companies have become more stringent with their on-site work policies, including hybrid work options.

Remote work policies may specify core working hours during which employees must be available online, even if they have flexible start and end times. They might also outline expectations for regular check-ins with managers, participation in virtual meetings, and timely responses to emails and messages. Additionally, these policies often include guidelines for maintaining a secure work environment, such as using company-approved devices, following data encryption protocols, and regularly updating software to protect against cyberthreats. Employers have also implemented measures to ensure that remote work does not compromise productivity. These measures can include setting clear performance metrics, using project management tools to track progress, and encouraging regular communication within teams. By adhering to these guidelines, employees can demonstrate their commitment to maintaining productivity and contributing to the company's goals, even while working remotely.

Following your company's remote work policies helps you integrate smoothly into the remote work environment and ensures that you remain aligned with the company's expectations and standards. Ignoring these policies can lead to misunderstandings, reduced productivity, and potential security risks, which can have serious consequences for both you and the organization.

Remote work policies are designed to create a structured and secure working environment. By adhering to these policies, you can avoid potential pitfalls and contribute effectively to your team's success, whether you're working from home or in a hybrid setup.

Dress Code Policies

Another common area of misunderstanding is an organization's dress code policy. Although it might seem that the corporate world has shifted toward more casual attire, influenced by leaders like Steve Jobs and Mark Zuckerberg, most companies have dress codes and expect employees to follow them. Understanding and adhering to the dress code is crucial in any organization. Dress codes reflect company culture and values and help you make a positive first impression. They ensure that employees present themselves in a professional manner, which can enhance the company's image and foster a sense of unity and belonging among staff. For new hires, following the dress code can help you integrate more smoothly into the workplace. It shows that you respect the company's standards and are committed to fitting in with the team. Additionally, dressing appropriately can boost your confidence and help you feel more prepared to tackle your new responsibilities. By aligning with the dress code, you contribute to a professional and cohesive work environment, which can positively impact your career progression.

If you interviewed on-site for your role, you might have already observed what your colleagues are wearing. That is the first place to start and learn about what is expected. I had worked in several Fortune 500 companies before I joined a smaller SaaS company based in San Francisco. My usual dress code on my first day is dress pants, blouse, and a professional blazer. Since I was going to be in San Francisco, I wanted to make sure I had a good layer on. I took the train to work so I decided to wear sneakers because I knew there would be a good amount of walking. But to be on the safe side, I also carried a pair of heels, since I was not sure what was expected. I knew I wanted to dress to impress because first impressions matter. As soon as I got out of the elevator, I went to the restroom and changed into my heels and fixed my makeup and my hair (San Francisco weather can be brutal). A wonderful person at reception greeted me, as I was early for my first day. I was seated in the lobby as they were getting my badge and onboarding package, and I started seeing an influx of employees arrive. Several wore jeans and sneakers and carried backpacks.

My manager met me in the reception area and started giving a walking tour of the company. Before this moment, I had only met him via Zoom. I enjoyed meeting him in person but noticed he too wore jeans, sneakers, and a casual jacket. We stopped in the middle of one of the corridors and he said, "Oh, there is the CEO. We should say hi to him." Several people were walking toward us. One man raised his hand to wave a hello, and it took me a few minutes to realize he was the CEO. He wore a sweatshirt, torn jeans, and worn sneakers. (This was a $2 billion company, so these clothes were a fashion statement.) We spoke for a few minutes, and my boss continued with the tour.

Guess what I did the next day? I wore my casual clothes and felt I was part of this new culture. I mixed and matched my attire, depending on what type of meetings and day I had, but mainly wore casual clothing. I can tell you, I didn't miss wearing my painful high heels while working there. I hope this example shows you that the dress code sometimes is not shared readily, and you have to observe. When in doubt, you can always ask your boss to be sure.

Types of Dress Codes

- **Business formal** is the most formal dress code, suitable for high-level meetings and special events.

    Examples: Tailored suits, dress shirts, formal dresses, and closed-toe shoes

- **Business professional** is traditional business attire that balances formality and comfort.

    Examples: Tailored suits, dress pants, blouses, dress shoes, and conservative accessories

- **Smart casual.** A blend of professional and casual wear.

    Examples: Blazers with jeans, collared shirts, skirts or dresses without excessive embellishments, loafers, and ankle boots

- **Business casual.** Comfortable professional attire for everyday office wear.

  Examples: Khakis, dress shirts, sweaters, cardigans, loafers, and closed-toe shoes

- **Casual:** Relaxed clothing suitable for creative industries, start-ups, or casual Fridays.

  Examples: Jeans, T-shirts, sneakers, and casual footwear

This Dress Code section is based on my experience and research for companies mostly in the United States. I also want to share that you must be highly sensitive and conscious of different regions where you might be working or have customers. For example, anyone who has worked in Japan knows that the dress standards are different there, and employees *and* customers are expected to adhere to a certain dress code. My husband, who is an executive leader for an engineering team, usually dresses in business casual. However, for his first visit to Japan, he researched the best way to be presentable and was advised to carry formal blazers and dress shoes. When he returned from his trip, he shared that he was glad he had taken extra blazers and that he would have felt out of place if he hadn't. By respecting cultural norms, it was easier for him to have business conversations with colleagues in Japan.

Ensuring Professionalism and Integrity with the Code of Conduct

Please note: This section offers an example of what a code of conduct document or process could look like in your organization. Yours might have more topics.

A Code of Conduct outlines the expected behavior and ethical standards within a company. The document serves as a guide for all employees to ensure a respectful, professional, and legally compliant work environment.

The next example presents an expanded overview to help new hires understand and adhere to these important guidelines.

- **Professional Interactions**
  - **Colleagues.** Treat all colleagues with respect and courtesy. Foster a collaborative and inclusive work environment by valuing diverse perspectives and contributions.
  - **Clients and stakeholders.** Maintain professionalism in all interactions with clients and stakeholders. Ensure clear, honest, and respectful communication to build and sustain trust.
- **Ethical Standards**
  - **Integrity.** Always act with integrity and honesty in all business dealings. Avoid any actions that could be perceived as deceitful or unethical.
  - **Confidentiality.** Protect sensitive company information and respect the privacy of colleagues and clients. Do not disclose confidential information without proper authorization.
- **Harassment and Discrimination**
  - **Zero tolerance.** The company has a zero-tolerance policy toward harassment and discrimination of any kind. These types of policies include, but are not limited to, harassment based on race, gender, sexual orientation, religion, or disability.
  - **Reporting.** If you experience or witness any form of harassment or discrimination, report it immediately to your supervisor or the HR department. The company is committed to investigating all reports thoroughly and confidentially.

- **Conflicts of Interest**
  - **Disclosure.** Avoid situations where personal interests could conflict with professional responsibilities. If a potential conflict arises, disclose it to your supervisor or the HR department immediately.
  - **Decision making.** Ensure that all business decisions are made in the best interest of the company, free from personal bias or gain.
- **Compliance and Consequences**
  - **Adherence.** Following the Code of Conduct is mandatory for all employees. Familiarize yourself with the document and ensure your actions align with its guidelines.
  - **Consequences.** Violating the Code of Conduct can result in serious consequences, including disciplinary action, termination, or legal repercussions. Understand that these measures are in place to maintain a safe and ethical workplace.
- **Onboarding and Acknowledgment**
  - **Training.** The Code of Conduct is a key component of the onboarding training for all new hires. This training ensures that every employee understands the company's expectations and their role in upholding these standards.
  - **Acknowledgment.** At the end of the onboarding process, employees are required to sign a document confirming that they have read, understood, and agree to comply with the Code of Conduct. This acknowledgment is crucial in reinforcing the importance of these guidelines.

    By following the Code of Conduct, you contribute to a positive and productive work environment.

Other Policies You May Encounter

Each organization is different and will have different sets of policies. Some additional policies to keep an eye on are discussed next.

IT and Data Security Policies

IT and data security policies outline the proper use of company technology and data. They include guidelines on password management, data encryption, and acceptable use of company devices and networks. Noncompliance can lead to data breaches, loss of sensitive information, and potential legal issues. In Strategy #4: Navigating Technology in Your New Role, I highlight key areas to monitor, emphasize the importance of following the rules, and remind you to always double-check with your manager.

Health and Safety Policies

Health and safety policies aim to maintain a secure working environment and outline procedures for handling emergency situations, identifying and mitigating workplace hazards, and adhering to health protocols. Ignoring these policies can lead to accidents, injuries, and legal liabilities for both employees and the company. For example, at Micron, where I previously worked, health and safety were taken very seriously at all levels. With over 17 global locations and a significant portion of the workforce in manufacturing spaces, adhering to safety protocols was essential. Employees working on the manufacturing floor needed to be certified to operate large machines and navigate the manufacturing areas safely. Safety was ingrained into the company culture from day 1. Regardless of the team or global location, every new hire underwent comprehensive safety and health training. This training was both mandatory and also regularly updated to ensure ongoing compliance and awareness. The training covered everything from emergency procedures to proper use of equipment and safe movement within the manufacturing areas. Micron's campuses featured extensive facilities with long corridors and numerous staircases, in both manufacturing and office spaces. To ensure that everyone adhered to safety rules, the company employed various communication methods. Corridor signage, digital displays, and regular news flashes via email and other channels were used to keep safety top of mind for all employees. By embedding safety into the company's DNA and making it a priority from the very beginning, Micron was able to create a safer, more efficient working environment. This approach protected employees and minimized legal risks while enhancing overall productivity. Ignoring such policies could have led to severe consequences, including accidents, injuries, and potential legal issues.

Leave and Time-off Policies

These policies detail the procedures for requesting and taking leave, including vacation, sick leave, and other types of time off. Not following these policies can lead to misunderstandings about your availability, disruptions in team planning, and potential conflicts with HR. Most companies that I have worked in have a documented policy of time off. Unfortunately, when you join a company, you usually start at zero hours of time off, and the amount slowly builds up each month. Many companies have different types of perks concerning time off; in some, you can also request as part of your offer to add a few hours of time-off so that you are not starting at zero. This perk is highly beneficial for new employees who might have upcoming vacation plans or medical appointments or for anyone who knows they will need to take time off for family-related issues. On your first day of orientation, you should receive information on the company's time-off policy. If you don't see that policy documented anywhere, talk to either your direct hiring manager or your HR business partner.

Official time-off policies are one way that companies help employees to balance their well-being, but other types of time-off policies exist. Several years ago, when I worked in San Francisco, the company that I had joined had removed restrictions on time off. Limitless time off was allowed. The company HR leader recommended that the best course was for employees to talk to their boss and team to confirm that no projects would be delayed if a person took time off and that there was always someone in the team to be the backup. Although the intention was good, this policy was very confusing, especially for new employees. I could not rely on a documented process but rather had to pray and hope that my boss would understand my situation before I could ask for a day off. Although this process might work for some, I felt the interpretation of who can take time off was completely dependent on their bosses. I share this story not to judge the time-off policy but to make you aware of such policy structures and suggest that you might need to plan for your own well-being.

Budget Policies

If you are the owner of your budget in your new role, you will need to learn the business cycle of your organization. Does the company follow a calendar cycle or a fiscal-year cycle? In which month does the fiscal year start? I have seen a wide variety of timelines. Some companies start their budget planning one quarter before the close of the current fiscal year, and they lock it down for the upcoming fiscal year. Sometimes companies lock down the budget plan strictly, and sometimes they are open to changes as the leaders want. There is no right or wrong way, but you need to be aware of the cycle. In my own experience, years ago when I worked for a mid-size company in San Francisco, I did not budget well. By not planning in advance, I missed team meetings in Asia because we had used up the travel budget before the end of the fourth quarter. I share this story to show the importance of staying ahead of budgeting while learning from your mistakes.

Travel Policies

If you are taking on a new role as a senior leader in your organization, travel might be a big part of your strategic plan.

Travel will help you get a good sense of your global team members and give you a chance to hear directly from your customers and business partners. Do your research on your company's internal website or in the documentation to read about their current travel policies within your country and to different countries. During COVID, many companies modified their travel policies and created stricter guidelines, and other unforeseeable conditions could create changes. Be sure to stay updated.

Business travel, though often seen as routine, plays a pivotal role in organizational dynamics. It facilitates knowledge exchange and learning by allowing us to break free from our familiar surroundings, much like our ancestors who journeyed to explore the unknown. From a business-specific perspective, understanding the company's business model reveals how value is created, delivered, and captured. With this knowledge, employees can align their efforts with organizational goals, making informed decisions second nature. Career advancement is another benefit, as a deep understanding of the business model unlocks growth and innovation, allowing employees to shape the company's future and drive sustainable growth. In addition, organizations must communicate risk exposures to employees. Business travel isn't just about flights and hotels; it's about expanding horizons, forging connections, and propelling success.

- **Finance liaison.** As a team or people leader, you or your function will have an assigned finance liaison. Meet with this liaison in your first 90 days to learn the budget cycle process. This person will guide you in this process and can teach you the unwritten rules. Sometimes you will have wiggle room for adding or editing budget line items; your finance partner can let you know what is acceptable in your company.

- **Inherited budget line items.** This was my blind spot, and I didn't pay attention to inherited budget line items as I took the people leader role during my time at SanDisk. Within a week of starting my new role, my boss moved on to another company. As a result, I had to take on the learning curve of my new role along with my former leader's role and his team. I was lucky to be in the right place at the right time, but I was saddled with committed projects and unexpected budget planning. I was good at planning for the upcoming quarter but didn't realize we had ongoing payments for several vendors that we managed centrally in my team. This was a hiccup in our planning. Thankfully, my new leader, the CPO, caught this and helped me to keep an eye on the budget process until I was up and running.

Communication Process

Ann, an experienced project manager, joined her new company when it was ramping up and hiring several new employees. Hiring went by fast and onboarding was a breeze. Since Ann had 10 years of experience, her boss didn't spend too much time onboarding her. He thought she was experienced enough, and she felt the same way. All the basics and checklists were given to Ann. Within the first 30 days, she had completed all of them and felt confident in her next steps. She had started working on a key project within the first 15 days of joining the company. She was juggling a lot.

While she was helping with the new project, she came across an urgent issue that required clarification, and she sent an instant message (IM) to her boss. She had noticed in the past that he used IM a lot with his team to give timely updates, so she used the same method. Half an hour went by, and he didn't respond. In her experience, if an urgent issue came up at work that needed approval to make a decision, she would request that from the next-level leader. She did the same here and sent an IM to her skip-level boss, who was the VP of the team. He responded within 10 minutes with approval. She moved forward in the next step of her project planning. Toward the end of the week, she had her weekly one-on-one meeting planned with her boss, and he checked in with her on her progress. She was excited to give all the updates on her projects and the people she connected with so far. As they were approaching the end of the meeting, her boss looked at her seriously, and the energy in the room shifted. He calmly told her that her reaching out directly to his boss was not the right process or communication escalation path in this company. He spent the last 10 minutes of their session explaining the communication escalation path for any approvals that were needed. He gave this feedback in a clear and kind manner and apologized for not making the process clear earlier. Ann felt bad about her actions but went on to follow the process and focus on the success of her new role.

Key Aspects of an Effective Communication Escalation Path

The communication escalation path outlines the channels and steps for resolving issues or making decisions within an organization while ensuring that problems are addressed promptly and with clarity.

The communication escalation path defines the boundaries and decision-making channels across the organization. It clarifies who is responsible for what type of decision, ensuring efficient problem solving.

Visual representations, such as escalation diagrams, depict the communication path. These diagrams show the responsibility chain, follow-up procedures, and notification routes. They help streamline decision making and prevent bottlenecks.

Steps in a Communication Escalation Process

Having defined steps in a communication escalation process ensures that urgent issues are addressed promptly and efficiently, preventing delays that could impact operations or decision making. It also provides clarity on roles and responsibilities, reducing confusion and fostering accountability within teams. Consider the next six steps.

1. **Identify the required decision or action.**

   Clarify needs. Determine the specific decision or action that management needs to take. Clearly outline the issue and the desired outcome to ensure precise and effective resolutions.

2. **Establish service-level agreements.**

   Set expectations. Define clear ground rules for response times and service expectations. These service-level agreements serve as a guide for your team and customers, ensuring everyone understands the timelines and standards during support interactions.

3. **Plan for escalation scenarios.**

   Anticipate triggers. Identify potential triggers that might necessitate an escalation. Recognize critical situations that require intervention from higher levels of expertise or authority to prevent issues from escalating further.

4. **Develop a customer communication protocol.**

   Ensure transparency. Establish a clear communication plan for interacting with customers during escalations. Determine how and when to communicate updates, ensuring transparency and empathy to keep customers informed and reassured.

5. **Define resolution criteria.**

   Set clear criteria. Determine the criteria for when an escalation is considered resolved. Clearly document what constitutes adequate resolution to avoid any ambiguity and ensure all parties are aligned on the outcome.

6. **Implement a postescalation process.**

   Follow-up steps. After resolving the issue, outline the necessary follow-up steps. Steps include closing tickets, gathering feedback from customers, and analyzing the escalation to learn and improve future processes.

Treat company processes as your treasure map. Each step reveals hidden gems—opportunities for growth, impact, and career advancement.

By following these steps, you can ensure a structured and effective escalation process that maintains high standards of customer service and operational efficiency. Treat company processes as your treasure map. Each step reveals hidden gems—opportunities for growth, impact, and career advancement.

Career Pointers

1. What policies do you need to learn more about at your new company (health, leave, IT, other)? Write down any questions you have for your manager or HR.

2. Start with your manager, access HR resources, and observe in order to learn more about your company's policies.

3. If you accidentally break a policy, communicate with your manager about it.

4. What are a few ways you'll benefit from understanding company processes?

Navigating Technology in Your New Role

Technology is the campfire around which we tell our stories.
—Laurie Anderson

WHEN JONATHAN STARTED HIS NEW role as a project manager for a software product company, his director asked him to create a 30-day plan to meet with all product owners to understand their milestones, deliverables, and key challenges. Doing this would help Jonathan to focus on Strategy #1 to meet the key people and also help him understand the short-term and long-term goals of his stakeholders. This request was straightforward. In his director's mind, this was the right thing to do to make Jonathan successful in his new role. But then Jonathan encountered a major challenge. On his third day on the job, his director went on an unplanned leave.

Jonathan had a great start on the first-day orientation from his HR team. His peers took him out for lunch and acquainted him with the building, the surroundings, and the key people. However, when it came to building his 30-day onboarding plan to understand the different product lines he would be supporting, Jonathan had no leads beyond one or two names shared by his director. He asked his nearby colleagues but didn't get a clear picture of who the key stakeholders were, which team or function they reported to, or where they were located geographically. Jonathan was a project manager who was supposed to set up global calls for these product lines, but he didn't know where to start.

As you are reading this, I'm sure you want to tell Jonathan: "Hey, why don't you start by logging into your laptop and looking for information within your company's intranet?" Jonathan thought of this and wanted to start browsing what systems and apps his company had, but he was nervous. In his 10-year career at another company, he had used Microsoft products; his new company used only Google products. Instead of trying to learn the new apps and get the information he needed, Jonathan froze.

You might think exploring new systems is easy, yet as I interviewed people for this book, I was surprised to learn how much apprehension people feel about new technology or learning how to navigate through company systems to expedite their own learning process. This apprehension holds them back and slows down their assimilation process in the organization.

When you join a new organization, chances are it uses different systems than your previous organizations to communicate, to set up meetings, to reach out to each other for urgent requests, and to manage people-related issues. If you are in a technical role, there might be different ticketing systems for working with IT and to manage ticketing within your own product updates and different links or websites internally within your company's firewalls for accessing information, documents, and managing approval processes.

As you explore the upcoming sections, you will find practical strategies and insights on leveraging company platforms and technology to accelerate your learning and boost efficiency. By embracing these tools, you can integrate seamlessly into your new environment, enhance collaboration, and set yourself up for success in your role.

Navigating a Virtual Workplace: Susan's Story

In the midst of the pandemic, Susan started a new professional journey. Her role demanded adaptability and resourcefulness, especially since she joined her team remotely. Without the luxury of face-to-face interactions, Susan turned to technology to bridge the gap.

- **Seeking information.** Susan read her company's internal blogs, mining them for insights about her team, manager, and colleagues. Result: These virtual glimpses provided context and helped her understand the dynamics at play.

- **Mastering the tools.** Susan immersed herself in Microsoft's suite of products, since that is what her company used. She explored organizational charts within her system, unraveling the intricate web of reporting structures. Result: This knowledge was pivotal for her role as an employee and safety specialist because it provided her the knowledge of whom to contact when she wanted to move her process along faster. Mastering platforms and tools is especially crucial in larger companies where sometimes, due to stronger policies and approval processes, projects become stuck in a loop.

- **Emailing strategically.** Armed with information, Susan crafted thoughtful meet-and-greet emails. She reached out to her colleagues, fostering connections despite the physical distance. Result: Her proactive approach set a positive tone for collaboration.

- **Engaging with stakeholders.** Recognizing the importance of senior leaders' decision making, Susan proactively scheduled introductory meetings. Result: By understanding reporting lines, she streamlined communication and accelerated her integration into the team.

Susan's story exemplifies how technology, curiosity, and adaptability can transform challenges into opportunities. Her virtual journey paved the way for effective collaboration, even when corridors remained unexplored.

Learning About Your New Company's Systems: Mary's Story

When Mary started her new job as a business analyst, one of the first things on her list was to learn more about the systems her company used. She talked to her peers and realized that Microsoft Teams (MS Teams) was the main portal and preferred platform for communication for her global team. She went to YouTube and studied videos on the best way to use MS Teams. As she explored the tool, she realized she could use the platform to add documents or files that were relevant to specific teams.

Her research led her to figure out several ways of connecting other Microsoft applications within one group chat. For instance, within her team, a small group of people were avid runners. They were talking about trying to catch a good run, but they were never able to make concrete plans due to everyone's schedules or the lack of timely communication. Mary took that as an opportunity to create an MS Teams Runners Group, added the key people she knew who were interested, and started adding messaging, ideas, and resources to get the group talking. Within two weeks, they had already done two runs before work and were making bigger plans for an ongoing effort to create competing teams to make it fun. This group started with five people. By the end of the first quarter, several other people were added by word of mouth, and they had close to 50 members. This experience of learning about the company's preferred platform or technology application helped Mary to learn a new system and also helped her to fit into the culture of the company and feel happy to be surrounded by new friends.

Standing Out by Embracing New Technology: My Story

Decades ago, I started a job managing technology systems, and learning those systems excited me even more than learning about the company's people and business. Our company recently launched the self-service platform Microsoft SharePoint, where functional teams could create their own SharePoint pages to provide team information and training materials and access documents.

I had joined a team of 20 people. Within a month of my hire, I was the first person in that group to learn SharePoint. I still remember my hiring manager praising me on how quickly I had learned the new system. I was already helping my other team members to learn and build informational pages for their work, too.

These days, SharePoint is present in the everyday life of employees. Through the years, companies like Microsoft and Google, among many others, have made it extremely easy for employees to learn and build their websites. However, when I started using this tool, building websites was a big feat. To be honest, I didn't do it for recognition. As a young employee, I was eager to learn and see outcomes from my work. I also think, as I was a recent graduate, I was exposed to more technology apps than the peers in my team at that time. By learning the new technology, I was able to expedite into my new role faster and was able to establish myself as the go-to person for all things SharePoint.

Are You an Early Adopter?

The theory of early adopters is part of the technology adoption life cycle, which outlines how different groups embrace new technologies over time. The sociologist Everett Rogers shared these ideas in his 1962 book, *Diffusion of Innovations* (Rogers 1962). This groundbreaking publication has become a key resource for understanding the spread of new ideas and technologies within societies and organizations. The technology adoption life cycle includes these stages: innovators, early adopters, early majority, late majority, and laggards.

- **Innovators** are the first group to adopt a new technology. They are risk takers and often have a high level of technical expertise.

- **Early adopters** are opinion leaders who are quick to adopt new technologies, second only to innovators.

- **Early majority** adopts new technology after seeing its benefits demonstrated by early adopters. Members of the early majority are more deliberate and cautious in their approach.

- **Late majority** individuals are skeptical and adopt new technology only after it has been widely accepted and proven.

- **Laggards** are the last group to adopt a new technology.

Early adopters play a role in the adoption process by providing valuable feedback to vendors, helping to refine product features, design, and support. In the corporate world, early adopters are vital for the successful implementation of new technologies. Understanding and leveraging the role of early adopters can be particularly beneficial for new hires. Early adopters are usually the first to try out new tools and systems and can offer insights and guidance on how to use these technologies effectively. They help new hires understand the benefits and potential challenges of the new technology, making the transition smoother. Do you see yourself as an early adopter?

Consider Communication Preferences

Although several of the apps, platforms, and options available in your new company may be new to you, you should discuss the preferred method for communication with your direct manager and your team members. Don't be alarmed if you hear different things from your manager and your team. It boils down to two things: personal preference and decision making through communication. Let me elaborate on both these points.

When I worked for a well-established hardware company with a 20-year legacy, it had long-tenured employees who had been there for many years. These employees had specific ways of making decisions and communicating as a team. They preferred all communication—approvals, project updates, team recognitions, and personal updates—via email. If the communication didn't come via email but through other means, such as an instant message, verbal communication, or any other means, it was not considered official. In contrast, when I joined an SaaS company where the employee demographic was between 25 and 40 years of age, I was inundated with communication through instant messaging on MS Teams, Slack, emails, and direct phone calls. Several decisions were made fast and with less red tape. Through the years, I realized that even though I might have my own preference on how to communicate at the workplace, at the end of the day, I need to clarify the preferences of my boss. For instance, although the SaaS company had direct messaging as the way to communicate, my manager there did not prefer that. I realized this very late. When I sent him messages via MS Teams, I could see he had read them but he would not reply.

Sometimes, when I asked for quick decisions and support on certain projects and there was silence on the other end, I would run through all the possible bad scenarios in my head and lose sleep. Later the manager would approve my request via an email. Through trial and error, I figured out that email was his preferred way of communication. Allow me to save you time and give you an easy way to understand this dynamic.

In your first one-to-one meeting with your manager, ask for their communication method or if there is an escalation path for communication. For instance:

- Use Slack or MS Teams for a quick project update, question, or personal update.
- Use email communication for writing to several stakeholders and partners for confirmation of a decision or approval.
- Call someone if an urgent decision needs to be made by the team or is requested by the customer.

Securing up-front clarification is essential for maintaining alignment between you and your manager. As you engage with stakeholders, absorb information, and navigate various company processes, these initial guidelines will serve as your compass. By establishing a shared understanding from the outset, you'll pave the way for effective collaboration and seamless integration.

Understand IT and Security Protocols

As a new hire, understanding and adhering to IT and data security policies helps you to protect the integrity, confidentiality, and availability of your company's technology and data.

Proper Use of Company Technology and Data

Use company technology and data exclusively for business purposes, ensuring that any personal use is minimal and does not interfere with work responsibilities. Additionally, be aware that company devices and networks may be monitored to ensure compliance with these policies.

Password Management

To ensure the security of company accounts, create strong, unique passwords that include a mix of letters, numbers, and special characters. Update your passwords and avoid reusing passwords across different accounts. Confidentiality is paramount, so never share your passwords with anyone. If you suspect that your password has been compromised, report it immediately and change it without delay.

Data Encryption

Safeguard sensitive data by encrypting it both in transit and at rest, covering emails, files, and all forms of data transmission. Utilize company-approved encryption tools and software to ensure secure protection.

Acceptable Use of Company Devices and Networks

Be sure to follow IT policies, which include creating strong, unique passwords, regularly updating them, and maintaining the confidentiality of login credentials. Company technology and data should be used exclusively for work-related tasks, with awareness that devices and networks may be monitored to ensure compliance.

Noncompliance and Consequences

Noncompliance with IT and data security policies can lead to severe consequences, such as data breaches, loss of sensitive information, and potential legal issues. Additionally, violations of these policies may result in disciplinary action, which could include termination of employment. When in doubt, check with your hiring manager, your peers, and, most important, the IT team. Most IT teams have a key person to contact or an email you can use. Keep this contact information handy.

My Uncomfortable Story About IT and Data Security

By adhering to your company's IT and data security policies, you play a role in protecting your company's technology and data assets. When I joined Palo Alto Networks, a leading cybersecurity company, I experienced firsthand its commitment to security—not just for customers but for employees as well.

As a new hire, I received the standard training that many organizations provide. However, Palo Alto Networks had a unique approach to educating new employees about security. On my first day, while sifting through welcome emails from peers and team members, I encountered one with the subject line: "Shveta, new hire—click here." I didn't recognize the sender, but since I didn't really know anyone in the organization, I thought this must be one of those onboarding emails. Today you might instinctively think, "Don't click." However, this wasn't common knowledge at the time. Naturally, I clicked, assuming the message was necessary for my onboarding. The message revealed: "This is a Phishing attack. Reach out to the IT team to learn more."

Initially I was nervous, thinking I had made a mistake on my first day. But I soon realized it was a clever tactic to make the lesson memorable and encourage further training on the topic. This is a great example of how Palo Alto Networks has maintained its leadership in the cybersecurity space through strategic policies and a strong alignment with customer needs.

Sci-Fi Becomes Reality: Artificial Intelligence and the Workplace

I've been an ardent fan of the sci-fi television series *The X-Files* for years. As a child, the show stood as the pinnacle of coolness on

Indian television—a beacon of mystery, intrigue, and uncharted territories. I was also impressed by the areas the stories delved into, the mysteries they tried to solve, and the interesting concepts they discussed. From an episode called "Ghost in the Machine," I first heard about the concept of artificial intelligence (AI). In the episode, an automated building starts killing anyone who goes against its agenda. The building could understand voice commands and help around the office. Of course, the plot line was a bit scary, but the thought that machines can learn and make decisions for humans was unimaginable at the time. I didn't believe that would ever happen in my lifetime. This episode was aired in 1993, ahead of its time. Now most of us have voice command technology somewhere in our homes, cars, or work environment. This technology helps us to multitask and plan things around our home and work. Due to new technological upgrades, we do not feel like we are talking with a machine. Chances are, either in your current company or the new company you will join, AI is already in use as a platform, system, or technology.

The phrase "AI in the workplace" refers to the integration of computer systems or machines that can simulate human intelligence. These intelligent systems perform tasks that once required human cognition, such as learning, problem solving, and decision making. The impact of AI spans various aspects of work, the economy, and our personal lives.

How to Use AI for Enhanced Efficiency

- **Automate planning.** Use AI-powered planning tools to optimize your schedule, allocate time effectively, and prioritize tasks based on workload and habits. These tools analyze data to provide personalized recommendations, helping you manage your time more efficiently.

- **Chatbots for assistance.** AI chatbots like ChatGPT can handle repetitive tasks, summarize content, and assist with brainstorming ideas. They're useful for writers, developers, and business professionals.

- **Transcription and note taking.** This tool helps to summarize important conversations. For example, Otter.ai is an AI assistant that transcribes audio in real time during virtual meetings and captures meeting slides.

- **Content creation and enhancement.** Tools like Jasper and Copy.ai can help generate headlines, blogs, and advertising copy. They enhance content creation by providing AI-generated suggestions.

- **Grammar checkers and rewording tools.** Grammarly, Wordtune, and ProWritingAid use AI to improve grammar, style, and readability in your writing. These tools help to refine documents and emails.

- **Video creation and editing.** Descript and Wondershare Filmora offer AI-driven video editing features. They streamline video production and enhance storytelling.

- **Image generation.** DALL·E 3 and similar tools can create unique images based on textual descriptions. These tools are useful for presentations, marketing materials, and social media.

- **Task and project management.** Asana, Any.do, and BeeDone use AI to streamline task management and collaboration and keep projects organized and on track.

- **Automation with Zapier.** Zapier allows you to create custom AI chatbots and automate actions without coding. It also helps to break down goals into actionable tasks using AI-powered bots.

In March 2024, I was privileged to present as a keynote speaker alongside esteemed figures such as Josh Bersin at the annual Irresistible conference at the USC Marshall School of Business campus in LA. A distinguished analyst, author, educator, and visionary in corporate talent, learning, and HR technology, Bersin possesses an intricate grasp of the global talent landscape, including the intricacies and evolving dynamics that influence corporate teams worldwide. His prolific contributions to HR technology literature consistently place him at the forefront of forecasting industry shifts. During the event, I engaged with numerous leaders from both domestic and international firms eager to demystify AI, explore its organizational applications, and identify focal areas for leaders to simplify AI adoption for their teams.

When my moment arrived to address the audience in a keynote session, Bill Pelster asked a thought-provoking question. He's a luminary in our domain and acted as the session's moderator. He asked, "In our profession, how do we stay abreast of artificial intelligence, and what should our learning trajectory entail?" I have over two decades of experience in human resources, and this question prompted a moment of introspection regarding AI's transformative impact on our professional duties and educational processes. These are the main ideas I shared.

- **Understand AI's true potential.** Separate fact from fiction when it comes to AI. By understanding the practical applications and limitations of AI, HR experts can harness the power of AI tools more effectively.

- **Continue to educate ourselves.** Staying abreast of AI innovations is a must for the HR sector. Doing this means committing to ongoing education and enhancing skills in areas related to AI.

- **Focus on AI ethics.** Confront issues like data protection and algorithmic bias head on. Training HR professionals in ethical AI practices will ensure that AI is used to promote equity and efficiency in HR procedures.

- **Adapt to new roles.** With AI taking over routine tasks, HR positions are set to change. Professionals need to be ready to assume roles that are more strategic and analytical, concentrating on domains with a necessary human touch.

Career Pointers

1. Think about whether you're an early adopter or not and how the answer might affect your work and communication style.

2. Note the communication preferences of your manager, direct reports, and colleagues.

3. Keep up on how your company uses, and plans to use, AI in the workplace.

4. Consider ways you can use AI in your daily work to improve your efficiency.

Know the Business

The more you understand about your company's business, the better you'll be able to contribute to its success.

—Indira Nooyi, CEO of Pepsi

THE ROOM WAS PACKED WITH students from all over the state. You could feel the excitement and hear the chess timer clocks clicking all around the room. The event was taking place in a big auditorium where all the state-level high school chess teams had come under one roof to take the title of the chess championship for 1993. I could feel all eyes on me as I walked into the semifinal round to represent my high school. I wore my school uniform with its red cardigan and school tie and polished black shoes. I won't say I walked in confidently, but I was not shy. I found my chair and sat in front of the chessboard, knowing well that this was a do-or-die situation. Within a few seconds, the name of my opponent was announced. When I looked around, I saw a guy much taller than me swagger over, pull out the chair across from me, and sit down. I would be lying if I didn't say I was not sweating. Although I was feeling anxious since the team depended on me, my focus was strong, and I had made up my mind. I planned to win.

The clock moved fast, and each one of us made our moves quickly and lost chess pieces to each other. Less than 10 minutes in, the game seemed to have lasted a year. I could hear the teams cheering each other and my name being called by my team members when I took my opponent's chess pieces. The chessboard slowly became emptier, and we just had a few pieces left. Every time he made a move, I studied the board to think through what his next two moves would be. Finally my opponent made a move that made me disbelieve what I was seeing. In my final move, I shifted my queen close to the king and said loudly, "Checkmate." My entire team and the auditorium burst into cheers. I was the last person standing to take our team to the finals. We'd done it.

That year, I was the newest member of the chess team. Someone had left the team, and it had a last-minute opening. I applied, and became the only girl on a six-boy team. My mom had taught me chess at the age of six. An avid player, she motivated me by giving me a Cadbury Chocolate bar if I could beat her. Through our many evening sessions, I had a lot of fun trying to win from her (and of course whining when I didn't). Over the years, I'd play with her, my uncles, and various local kids.

Although I had never played competitively, I always declared myself the chess champion in my neighborhood. But when I joined the high school chess team, my self-confidence was shaken. These kids were not just good; they were *very* good. They loved torturing themselves with the toughest games and loved spending hours learning. As the only girl on the team, fitting in was not easy. I felt part of the team when I was included in a city-level chess champion session for high schools, and I surprised my teammates by winning all my rounds. On the school bus going home after the tournament, they walked in and gave me a fist bump. That fist bump was the acknowledgment that I had made it. Twenty other kids had applied for that one open seat on the team, but I'd been able to display my strengths to the coach. I give the biggest credit to my mother.

My mother always encouraged me to plan, saying, "Always think two steps ahead." Since everyone else knows the same moves, the ability to think and plan ahead is what helps a player to win or lose. She taught me to consider what I could do to get back into the game when my best plans didn't work out. My mom gave me several chess books with various games and examples in them (this was before everything was available online). She inscribed the books with: "Don't leave anything to chance—prepare well." She taught me that knowing the technical aspects of the game is not enough. You need practice and the ability to fail fast and learn fast. In chess, your opponent, the availability of a team, and your own confidence in making the right moves make a difference. The metaphor of playing chess and planning two steps ahead offers valuable insights for planning well when taking on a new role.

Beginning a new job can feel like entering a strategic game like chess, where every move requires thought, adaptation, and a keen understanding of the playing field. The pieces are in place, and the game is about to begin. Just as a chess player combines foresight, adaptability, and psychological awareness, you too can apply these principles to navigate your new role successfully.

The Principles of Chess You Can Use to Navigate Your New Role

- **Anticipate moves.** In chess, thinking ahead is crucial. Similarly, in your new job, take time to understand the company's goals, your team's dynamics, and the challenges you'll face. Consider the long-term impact of your decisions. When in doubt, ask yourself: "What are the potential consequences of my actions? How can I align my work with the organization's vision?"

- **Be ready for surprises.** Chess players adjust their strategies based on their opponent's moves. Similarly, be flexible in your approach. Things won't always go as planned, and that's okay.

Embrace change, learn from setbacks, and be open to feedback. Adaptability is a key trait of successful professionals.

- **Understand people.** Chess involves reading your opponent's intentions. In your workplace, understand the motivations, communication styles, and personalities of your colleagues. Build strong relationships by actively listening, empathizing, and recognizing the unique strengths each team member brings.

- **Sharpen your skills.** Chess masters study past games, analyze patterns, and refine their techniques. Apply the same mindset to your job. Seek out learning opportunities: Attend workshops, read industry news, and stay curious. Invest in your growth.

- **Know the game.** Just as chess has rules, every organization has its business models, culture, and ways of doing things. If you want to be successful, you should learn these aspects, respect them, and contribute positively to your team and organization. Observe how decisions are made, how conflicts are resolved, and what values matter most. Align your behavior accordingly.

Your new role is like a chess game—a mix of strategy, adaptability, and human dynamics. Approach it with curiosity, resilience, and a willingness to learn.

Understand the Company's Business Model

For new employees, understanding their company's business model is akin to laying a solid foundation. It's the compass that guides their journey toward meaningful contributions and career growth. Let's explore why this knowledge matters.

- **Value creation and delivery.** By unraveling how the company creates, delivers, and captures value, employees gain clarity on their role within the larger ecosystem. Armed with this under-standing, they can align their efforts with organizational goals, ensuring their work contributes directly to success.

- **Informed decision making.** Research, observation, and questioning are key. New employees should delve into the intricacies of the business model. Armed with insights, they make informed decisions—whether it's optimizing processes, enhancing customer experiences, or driving innovation.

- **Unlocking opportunities.** A deep understanding of the busi-ness model reveals hidden opportunities. It's the gateway to innovation, efficiency, and expansion. As employees grasp these nuances, they position themselves for career advance-ment. They become architects of their own growth.

- **Valuable assets.** Employees who embrace the business model become more than team members; they're stewards of the company's destiny. Their insights drive sustainable growth and prosperity, ensuring the organization thrives in a dynamic landscape.

I have interviewed and worked with several engineers and knowl-edge workers who understand the product they are building for their company but don't understand how all the other functions in the company come together and work in cohesion. For roles in human resources, finance, IT, sales and marketing teams, consider the key products, your competitors in the industry, the business results for the last quarter, and your company's overall financials.

To gain insights into how leaders worldwide prepare for new roles, particularly from a business perspective, I spoke with Rob Beard, the chief legal officer, general counsel, and head of global policy at Mastercard. In this role, he oversees the company's pub-lic policy, regulatory affairs, and litigation teams globally and is a member of the Management Committee. At the time of our interview, Rob had been in his position at Mastercard for nearly a year, having recently transitioned from Micron Technology, a global semiconductor and manufacturing company.

Rob approached learning about his new company with a hands-on, experiential mindset. He began by immersing himself in extensive reading, devouring every available public document, including the company's annual reports, proxy statements, and strategy documents. This thorough research helped him understand the company's strategy and the broader industry context, especially as he transitioned from semiconductors to the payments industry. Rob also focused on understanding the geopolitical issues affecting the company, recognizing the importance of these factors in his role. Beyond reading, he engaged in numerous conversations, asking insightful questions and genuinely listening to understand the motivations and goals of his colleagues. This inquisitive approach allowed him to identify opportunities to contribute meaningfully without overstepping, ensuring he could support his team effectively while observing its dynamics. Overall, he stressed the importance of taking time to learn and understand the new environment, including its systems, processes, and people, before making significant changes. He believes in being deferential to the team's current methods and gradually building trust.

How to Understand the Business of Your Business

Understanding the key aspects of your company's business as a new hire enables you to align your work with its goals, make informed decisions, and contribute meaningfully from the start. It also helps you build credibility, foster collaboration, and quickly adapt to the company culture, setting a strong foundation for professional growth.

- **Explore the company website.** Check the "About Us" section, mission, and vision statements, and familiarize yourself with the products or services.

- **Read annual reports and press releases.** These documents provide insights into the company's financial health, goals, and recent achievements.

- **Engage with internal resources.** Use the intranet, newsletters, and training materials to learn about the company's operations and culture.

- **Network with colleagues.** Build relationships with peers, managers, and other departments to understand the company's processes and priorities.

- **Attend meetings and training sessions.** Participate in onboarding sessions, team meetings, and training programs to learn about strategies and workflows.

- **Ask questions.** Don't hesitate to ask about the company's history, market position, or specific processes. Doing so shows your eagerness to learn and adapt.

As you prepare to start your new role, create a checklist of topics you want to learn about your company's business model. During my discussions with several leaders and also while researching for this book, I realized that new employees become so focused on their own role that often they don't take the time to learn about the overall company and other functions. This is because organizations usually hire late. By that, I mean they hire when the workload has increased beyond capacity or only after an employee leaves a position. These situations create an urgency to hire, which means that the company wants new hires to be productive toward the company's bottom line as quickly as possible. Rarely do organizations plan way in advance, hire at the right time, and give new hires time to slowly get up to speed.

Early in my career when I joined a midsize organization, I was excited about the vision for it to grow fast. I didn't really understand what that meant and how fast things were moving in that organization. After the HR orientation on my first day, my hiring manager took me to lunch and then took me around the office to introduce leaders and team members. One of the most senior leaders stopped, said hello, and added, "It is great you have joined us, but we needed you to start yesterday." He laughed and walked away. I thought he was joking. I was completely wrong. They were happy to give me time for my first-day orientation, but after that, I was expected to learn on the go without taking much time to adjust. As one of my mentors used to say, "Take your time, but hurry up."

Know and Understand the Products and Services

You can learn about your company's products in various ways, including the ones discussed next.

- **Product training sessions.** Many companies conduct formal product training sessions for employees, especially new hires. These sessions may be led by product managers, subject matter experts, or experienced sales representatives and cover product features, benefits, use cases, and value propositions.

- **Online resources.** Explore your company's intranet, internal databases, or online learning platforms for resources related to your company's products. These resources may include product manuals, technical specifications, demo videos, FAQs, and case studies.

- **Shadowing.** Observing experienced colleagues, such as sales representatives or customer support agents, can provide valuable insights into how your company's products are marketed, sold, and supported. Observe customer interactions, product demonstrations, and troubleshooting processes to gain a better understanding of the products' features and functionalities.

- **Hands-on experience.** If possible, try to gain hands-on experience with your company's products. Depending on your role, you may have access to demo units, test environments, or product samples to explore the products firsthand and familiarize yourself with their capabilities.

- **Customer feedback.** Review customer feedback, testimonials, and reviews to gain insights into how customers perceive and use your company's products. Understanding customer pain points, preferences, and satisfaction levels can provide valuable context for learning about the products and identifying areas for improvement.

- **Cross-functional collaboration.** Collaborate with colleagues from other departments, such as marketing, product management, engineering, and customer support, to learn more about your company's products from different perspectives. Engage in discussions, attend meetings, and participate in cross-functional projects to gain insights into product development, marketing strategies, and customer feedback.

- **Industry research.** Stay informed about industry trends, the competitive landscape, and market dynamics related to your company's products. Reading industry publications, attending conferences, and participating in webinars can help you gain a broader understanding of the market and the context in which your company's products operate.

- **Continuous learning.** Commit to continuous learning and self-improvement. Set aside time to regularly review and update your knowledge about your company's products, staying informed about new features, updates, and developments. Take advantage of professional development opportunities, such as online courses, workshops, and certifications, to deepen your expertise and stay ahead of the curve.

By leveraging these concepts you can learn about your company's products and become a knowledgeable and valuable asset to your organization.

Review the Organizational Charts

As a new employee, the organizational chart can be a valuable tool for understanding the structure, hierarchy, and relationships within the company. Here's what to know about how to use the chart to your benefit.

- **Understand the reporting structure.** The organizational chart provides a visual representation of the reporting structure within the company, showing the relationships between different departments, teams, and positions. Use the chart to identify your direct supervisor as well as other key stakeholders you may interact with regularly. Understanding the reporting structure helps you know whom to go to for guidance, feedback, and approvals.

- **Identify key departments and functions.** Study the organizational chart to identify key departments and functions within the company, such as sales, marketing, finance, human resources, operations, and more. Understanding the roles and responsibilities of each department helps you gain insight into how the company operates and how different parts of the organization interact with each other.

- **Clarify roles and responsibilities.** The chart can help you clarify roles and responsibilities within your own team and across other departments. Doing this can help you understand how your role fits into the broader organizational structure and how your work contributes to the company's goals. It also allows you to identify potential collaborators and stakeholders for projects or initiatives.

- **Navigate communication channels.** The organizational chart can help you navigate communication channels within the company. Use it to identify key decision makers, influencers, and points of contact for different areas of the business. Doing so can be especially helpful when seeking information, resolving issues, or collaborating with colleagues from other departments.

- **Gain awareness of career paths.** Reviewing the organizational chart can give you insight into potential career paths and opportunities for advancement within the company. By understanding the hierarchy and progression paths, you can set goals for your career development and identify areas where you may want to gain experience or skills to advance.

- **Build relationships.** Use the organizational chart as a tool for networking and building relationships within the company. Reach out to colleagues in different departments or at similar levels in the hierarchy to learn more about their roles, experiences, and perspectives. Building a strong network within the organization can enhance collaboration, support, and career opportunities.

Overall, the organizational chart is a valuable resource for new employees to understand the structure, dynamics, and opportunities within the company. By leveraging the chart effectively, you can navigate the organization more confidently, collaborate more effectively, and position yourself for success in your role and career.

The Case for Stakeholder Mapping

In Strategy #2: Goal Setting and Feedback, I introduced the concept of stakeholder mapping with your hiring manager to help you build a 90-day plan of action and to meet the people who will be crucial in making you successful in your new role. This process can help with the next items.

- **Alignment and focus.** Understanding the business model enables employees to align their efforts with the company's strategic priorities and focus on activities that drive value creation. By prioritizing tasks and initiatives that directly contribute to the company's objectives, employees can optimize their impact and effectiveness in their roles.

- **Informed decision making.** Armed with knowledge of the business model, employees are better equipped to make informed decisions that support the company's long-term success. Whether it's evaluating new opportunities, mitigating risks, or resolving challenges, employees can apply their understanding of the business model to make sound judgments and choices.

While researching this book, I met with Cynthia Owyoung, the a human resources executive with over 20 years of experience. Her impressive journey spans leadership roles at Robinhood Financial, Charles Schwab, GitHub, and Yahoo, among others. As a longtime friend, I marveled at her seamless transitions between organizations. Naturally, I sought her wisdom. When we spoke, she highlighted the importance of working with people and building relationships, but one thing that stood out was the way she works with her stakeholders. She begins by conducting a stakeholder mapping exercise with her manager to define her initial list. When meeting each stakeholder, she asks, "Can you recommend two other people I should meet as I transition into this role? Who will support me or have a vested interest in the outcomes?" This strategy continuously expands and validates her stakeholder list, keeping it dynamic. She emphasized that organizations are built on people, and by planning, meeting, and building relationships, you can assimilate faster.

Cynthia's method is a testament to the power of strategic networking and building relationships. The dynamic process fosters both personal growth and professional success. Her insights remind us that by investing time in understanding and expanding our network, we can accelerate our assimilation and contribute more effectively to our new roles. This strategy is invaluable for anyone looking to navigate career transitions with confidence and purpose.

Career Pointers

1. Use the principles shared in this strategy to navigate your new role. Choose the ones that apply most to your situation.

2. Gain an understanding of the company's business model so you understand how you can contribute.

3. Use the steps shared in this strategy to understand the business of your business.

4. Research your company's products and services, and know them inside and out.

5. Use stakeholder mapping to help you achieve a deeper understanding of the organization.

The Company Culture

Culture is simply a shared way of doing something with a passion.

—Brian Chesky, CEO, Airbnb

CHIP KELLY, NFL COACH, gained prominence as the head coach of the University of Oregon football team, where he implemented an innovative and high-tempo offensive system known as the blur offense. His success at Oregon, characterized by a fast-paced, spread offense that emphasized speed and conditioning, garnered widespread attention and led to his hiring as head coach of the NFL's Philadelphia Eagles in 2013. In his first season with the Eagles, Chip Kelly's fast-paced offense took the NFL by storm, and the team finished with a 10–6 record, winning the NFC East division title. However, subsequent seasons saw diminishing returns as opposing teams began to adapt to Kelly's system, and the Eagles' performance declined.

In 2015, Chip Kelly's tenure as head coach of the Eagles ended after a disappointing 6–9 record. Kelly was hired as head coach of the San Francisco 49ers for the 2016 season. However, his fast-paced, up-tempo offensive system, which had worked well at Oregon and initially in Philadelphia, struggled to translate to long-term success in the NFL.

With the 49ers, Chip Kelly's offensive playbook failed to produce the desired results, and the team finished the 2016 season with a dismal 2–14 record, marking one of the worst seasons in franchise history. Despite his efforts to adapt and tweak his system, Kelly's inability to execute his high-tempo offense in the NFL led to his dismissal as head coach of the 49ers after just one season.

Kelly's experience serves as an example of how a coach's successful playbook in one setting may not necessarily translate to success in a different environment and underscores the importance of adaptability and flexibility. The same is true for new employees seeking to integrate themselves into a new environment.

Why Learning About a Company's Culture Matters

Learning about the company culture is essential for new employees to integrate into their new workplace, build relationships, enhance performance, make informed decisions, and contribute to the organization's success. The next list provides some specifics.

- **Integration and adaptation.** Understanding the company culture helps new employees integrate into their new workplace more smoothly. By learning about the shared values, norms, and practices of the organization, new employees can adapt their behavior and communication style to align with the company's expectations.

- **Building relationships.** Company culture influences how employees interact with one another and collaborate on projects. By familiarizing themselves with the company culture, new employees can build stronger relationships with their colleagues, managers, and other stakeholders. Doing this facilitates teamwork, communication, and cooperation across different departments and levels of the organization.

- **Performance and productivity.** A positive company culture that values transparency, open communication, and collaboration can enhance employee morale, engagement, and productivity. New employees who understand and embrace the company culture are more likely to feel motivated and empowered to contribute to the organization's success.

- **Decision making.** Company culture often shapes decision-making processes and priorities within an organization. By learning about the company culture, new employees gain insight into how decisions are made, what factors are considered important, and what values guide those decisions. This insight enables them to make informed choices and align their actions with the organization's goals and values.

- **Retention and job satisfaction.** Research shows that employees who feel a sense of belonging and alignment with the company culture are more likely to stay with the organization long term. By learning about and embracing the company culture, new employees can develop a stronger sense of loyalty, job satisfaction, and commitment to their roles.

- **Representing the brand.** Employees are often seen as ambassadors of the company's brand and values. By understanding and embodying the company culture, new employees can represent the organization's brand to external stakeholders, including customers, clients, partners, and the broader community.

- **Cultural fit.** Many organizations place importance on cultural fit when hiring new employees. By learning about the company culture during the onboarding process, new employees can assess whether they align with the organization's values, work environment, and expectations. This method helps both employees and the organization determine if there is a good fit for long-term success and satisfaction.

How to Find the Ideal Company Culture for You

In 2019, my family and I took our annual summer trip to our uncle's home in Los Angeles, which involved around six hours of driving. This tradition gave us invaluable time together as a family—time filled with lively conversation, storytelling, and the enjoyment of good music and snacks. During that trip, my husband and I discussed our careers, reflecting on our professional journeys and contemplating our future trajectories.

I confided in him about feeling stagnant in my current role, lacking the excitement that once fueled my workdays.

As our conversation continued, my husband asked, "Where do you envision yourself next? What criteria are essential for your next career move?" He handed me a small black notebook during a pit stop at a Starbucks, encouraging me to jot down the top qualities I sought in my next workplace. Here's what I wrote:

1. **Boss**—I want a boss who challenges me and gives me space to grow.

2. **Company**—I want to be part of a mission-focused company that is making a difference in the world by both creating innovative products and services and by believing in their employees.

3. **Coworkers and team**—I am a connector. I like being surrounded by people from whom I can learn, who enjoy working together, and who are willing to give their support for the success of their team.

4. **Strong leaders at the top**—In the world of HR or people teams, it is important to have the support of the top leaders in an organization because building strong employees, strong teams, and a strong company takes vision and execution from the top.

Without using the word "culture," I had written requirements that create the basic foundation of company culture. This list helped me to see that I was looking for a company that embraced a strong and healthy culture. This is a helpful exercise to guide you in the right direction, and the process worked well for me.

In my role as the head of global learning and development, I had the opportunity of working with leaders to build companies with strong cultures. Doing this included supporting employee learning opportunities, diversity initiatives, reducing red tape for approvals, among others. Several research studies have investigated how cultures are created or shaped in companies. An excellent read on this topic is Melissa Daimler's book, RE-CULTURING, where she explores practical approaches to redefining and strengthening workplace culture. In her work, Daimler emphasizes the importance of reculturing— an ongoing process that ensures a company's values and behaviors remain aligned as it evolves. She highlights three key areas for leaders to focus on: Purpose, which clarifies why an organization exists; Strategy, which defines what the company aims to achieve; and Culture, which shapes how employees work, behave, and interact. Through this framework, Daimler provides leaders with actionable insights to foster a more intentional and effective workplace environment.

What Is Meant by "Company Culture" Anyway?

According to Erin Meyer in the *Harvard Business Review* (2024), organizational culture can be defined as "the shared values, beliefs, and norms that influence how members of an organization interact with each other and interpret their environment." Organizational culture encompasses the unwritten rules, social norms, and behavioral patterns that shape the attitudes, behaviors, and experiences of employees within the organization. Several key elements often characterize organizational culture.

- **Values and beliefs** are the core principles and ideals that guide behavior and decision making within the organization. They reflect what the organization stands for and what it prioritizes, such as integrity, innovation, customer focus, or teamwork.

- **Norms and expectations** are the unwritten rules that govern behavior and interactions within the organization. They define acceptable and unacceptable behavior, communication styles, and work practices. Norms can vary across different departments, teams, and organizational levels.

- **Symbols and artifacts** are tangible manifestations of the organization's culture, such as the physical workspace, corporate branding, rituals, ceremonies, and traditions. They serve as visual cues and reminders of the organization's values and identity.

- **Behavioral patterns** are recurring patterns of behavior and interaction that characterize the organization's culture. They include how decisions are made, how conflicts are resolved, how feedback is given and received, and how success is celebrated.

- **Leadership** shapes and reinforces organizational culture. Leaders set the tone, model desired behaviors, and promote cultural values through their actions, decisions, and communication style. Employees look to leaders for guidance and inspiration in embodying the organization's culture.

- **Employee engagement and alignment** is fostered by a strong organizational culture that encourages high levels of employee engagement, commitment, and alignment with the organization's goals and objectives. Employees who resonate with the organization's culture are more likely to be motivated, productive, and satisfied in their roles.

Overall, organizational culture is a powerful force that influences employee behavior, attitudes, and performance and plays a critical role in shaping organizational identity, driving employee engagement, and impacting organizational success. Understanding and managing organizational culture helps leaders and managers create a positive and productive work environment and achieve strategic objectives.

Examples of Company Cultures and How They Look and Feel

Company cultures vary widely depending on factors such as industry, size, leadership style, geographic location, and organizational values. The next examples illustrate the variety of cultures across industries.

Google (Alphabet Inc.) is known for its innovative and collaborative culture, where employees are encouraged to think creatively, take risks, and collaborate across teams. The company's open office spaces, flexible work hours, and emphasis on employee perks and benefits promote a culture of creativity, experimentation, and inclusivity.

Zappos is renowned for its customer-centric culture, where employees are empowered to prioritize customer satisfaction above all else. The company's core values, such as "Deliver WOW Through Service" and "Embrace and Drive Change," guide employees in their interactions with customers and colleagues, fostering a culture of service excellence and continuous improvement.

Netflix has a high-performance culture characterized by a focus on results, accountability, and continuous learning. The company values transparency, candid feedback, and a culture of "freedom and responsibility," where employees are trusted to make autonomous decisions and take ownership of their work. Netflix's "Culture Deck," a widely circulated document outlining the company's values and principles, serves as a guiding framework for employees.

Southwest Airlines has a fun and customer-focused culture that prioritizes employee engagement, humor, and a "warrior spirit" mentality. The company's employees, known as Warriors, are encouraged to bring their personalities to work, have fun, and create memorable experiences for customers. Southwest's emphasis on employee empowerment and servant leadership contributes to a positive and supportive work environment.

Apple Inc. has a design-driven and innovative culture that prioritizes simplicity, elegance, and user experience. The company's design-centric approach, led by its late cofounder Steve Jobs, emphasizes creativity, attention to detail, and a relentless pursuit of excellence. Apple's commitment to confidentiality, coupled with its commitment to disruptive innovation, fosters a sense of excitement and anticipation among employees and customers alike.

These are just a few examples of company cultures, and each organization's culture is unique to its values, goals, and priorities. Regardless of the specific culture, a strong company culture aligns with the organization's mission, fosters employee engagement and well-being, and contributes to its long-term success.

Company Cultures That Failed

Several companies, such as those described next, have faced significant challenges or failed due to toxic or dysfunctional company cultures.

Once one of the largest energy companies in the world, **Enron** collapsed in 2001 due to a combination of accounting fraud, unethical practices, and a toxic corporate culture. The company's aggressive pursuit of profits at any cost, along with a culture of secrecy, fear, and intimidation, contributed to its downfall. Enron's collapse led to the loss of thousands of jobs, investor losses, and significant regulatory reforms.

Theranos was a biotech startup founded by Elizabeth Holmes with the promise of revolutionizing blood testing. However, the company's culture of secrecy, deception, and overpromising led to its downfall. Theranos falsely claimed that its technology could conduct comprehensive blood tests using a small amount of blood, leading to widespread media coverage and investor interest. When the technology failed to deliver on its promises, the company faced lawsuits and regulatory scrutiny before dissolving in 2018.

The company culture at **WeWork** faced significant criticism due to poor leadership, financial mismanagement, and unethical practices. Cofounder and former CEO Adam Neumann's erratic behavior and conflicts of interest, combined with rapid, unprofitable expansion, created financial instability. The chaotic work environment, marked by nepotism and favoritism, further undermined employee morale. These issues, along with Neumann's misuse of company resources, led to a toxic culture and ultimately contributed to WeWork's dramatic downfall.

These examples highlight the importance of ethical leadership and a transparent, supportive work environment.

Seven Ways to Gain Insight into a Company Culture

Understanding a company's culture is essential to ensure a good fit, satisfying career path, enjoyable work and colleagues, and fulfillment.

1. **Do your research.** Start by visiting the company's website. Look for information about its culture, values, and work environment. Pay attention to what is emphasized—whether it's work-life balance, collaboration, or growth opportunities.

2. **Check the news.** News articles, press releases, and any major events can provide insights into the company's culture, values, and direction.

3. **Ask specific questions.** During interviews or networking conversations, ask targeted questions about the company's culture. For instance:

   - How does the company support employee development?
   - What is the team dynamic like?
   - Are there any company traditions or rituals?

4. **Know yourself.** Reflect on your own preferences and values. Consider what aspects of a company's culture are important to you. Are you looking for a supportive environment, opportunities for growth, or a flexible work arrangement? Align your priorities with the company's culture to make an informed decision. When I wrote the list of elements that I was looking for in my role, the strongest value I sought was having coworkers and team members I can learn from and a boss interested in the team's success. During the interview process, I paid close attention to all my interviewers, especially my potential boss. I agreed to take on the role only when I knew the company and job would fulfill my priorities.

5. **Talk to current and former employees.** Reach out to people who work or have worked at the company. Use platforms like LinkedIn to connect with them. Ask about their experiences, work-life balance, team dynamics, and overall satisfaction. Their insights can provide valuable context. Keep your questions or messages professional and inquire about their thoughts on the organization. For example, you might say: "I'm considering an opportunity with company ABC and hoping to learn more about your experience working there." This step proved

invaluable as I was considering a lucrative offer from a company where I would have stepped into a previous leader's role to support the vision of the new chief people officer. My instincts told me something was off, so I reached out to a former colleague who had recently left the company for his candid insights. During our conversation, he shed light on the organizational changes and turmoil happening within the company, confirming that it wasn't the right environment for me at that stage of my career. In hindsight, I am grateful I declined the offer, as the company went through two leadership changes and was eventually acquired by another organization.

6. **Assess team dynamics.** Pay attention to how team members interact. Are they collaborative, supportive, and respectful? Team dynamics often reflect the broader organizational culture. Consider whether you feel comfortable in such an environment.

7. **Trust your gut.** Sometimes your intuition can guide you. If something feels off during the interview process or company interactions, trust your instincts. A mismatch in cultural fit can lead to dissatisfaction down the line. Contrary to popular belief, the word "culture" is not a buzzword. Although "company culture" may indeed be a term frequently used in business discussions, the impact of culture on organizational success cannot be overstated. It represents the intangible yet powerful elements that shape employee experiences, organizational dynamics, and the ability of the organization to achieve its strategic objectives. Therefore, rather than dismissing "culture" as a mere buzzword, leaders and organizations should recognize and prioritize the cultivation of a strong and positive company culture.

Tegwen, the vice president of human resources for a prominent retail company, has shared a profound insight into the importance of aligning personal values with a company's ethos. Her transition from a tech company to the retail industry underscores a strategic approach to career moves—prioritizing a deep understanding of an organization's core principles. Tegwen emphasizes the necessity of thorough preparation before starting a new role, advocating for a proactive stance in uncovering the essence of a company's culture and values.

By engaging with hiring managers and recruiters beyond surface-level inquiries, one can ascertain the true nature of a company's commitment to its employees and mission. If values are as important to you as they are to the company, ask relevant questions, including:

- How do the values show up in the company goals?
- How are decisions made in the company based around the values?
- What type of investment is made in employee development?

Ensure that the answers are satisfactory before you accept the role and make a move. Tegwen's advice serves as a valuable beacon for anyone navigating the waters of career transition. The goal is to find a harmonious match where one's personal convictions and a company's vision coalesce. This constructive collaboration fosters individual satisfaction while propelling the collective ambition of the organization. As you research new roles, let Tegwen's wisdom guide you to make informed decisions that resonate with your core beliefs, ensuring a fulfilling journey in your professional life.

What to Know About Company Culture and the New Employee

In his 2015 book *Work Rules*, Laszlo Bock provides insights from his tenure leading the human resources team at Google. He vividly describes the initial experiences of new Google employees, affectionately known as Googlers, upon stepping onto the campus for the first time. Amenities from sleeping pods to climbing walls, free food, and a plethora of events are certainly enticing. However, Bock emphasizes that while these perks are enjoyable, they only scratch the surface of Google's culture. Diving into the essence of the company's culture enables employees to make informed decisions and navigate their roles successfully beyond the superficial attractions.

Dov Seidman, a business leader who graduated from Oxford and Harvard, published his first book, *HOW* (2011), to highlight how things really happen in an organization and how company culture guides people's behaviors. According to Seidman, a company rulebook can tell its employees what to do and what not to do. However, employees need company culture to tell them what they *should* do. To Seidman's point, an employee handbook is one of the easiest ways of finding more information about the company culture and its policies. Usually an employee handbook is written from a legal perspective. Reading the handbook is a good start to learn about the company policies, what the stance is for social media, taking pictures on-site, speaking opportunities outside the organization, and others. For example, when new hires join a new organization, they might share photos or messages on social media with their network. This wasn't allowed in a manufacturing company. The employee who shared this news on social media received a strict warning from his boss the very next day and was asked to thoroughly review the employee handbook to avoid such mistakes.

The Culture at Amazon

Nithya Ruff and I first met at a brainstorming meeting to help employees learn about a technical topic when we both worked at SanDisk. I was leading the global learning and development team, and this was a topic I was passionate about. I was happy to see the same passion in Nithya, who at that time was representing one of the technical business units. Through the years, we have kept in touch as we have journeyed through various professional paths and continued learning from each other.

Her career trajectory has been great to see. She started her career at SGI in marketing and strategy and grew in different capacities in Avaya, Synopsis, and Comcast. When I was discussing this book idea with her, she shared examples of how she immersed herself in Amazon.

The Amazon culture is distinctive and robust, with its roots deeply embedded in the company's history and still actively embraced today. Amazon's leadership principles and various operational processes remain consistent throughout the different sectors of the company, forming the essence of leadership and daily operations. This culture is meticulously chronicled and integrated into onboarding processes as well as reinforced regularly over the course of the year. Nithya's own leadership capabilities were significantly enhanced by a comprehensive three-day training program, which provided a deep dive into the company's heritage and ethos. Mastery of the company's unique vernacular is essential for success, particularly in areas like open source that inherently operate in a different dialect. It's imperative to interpret and align open source initiatives with the company's objectives and linguistic framework to ensure they resonate. In contrast, other organizations she has been part of have struggled to define their culture as clearly or to infuse it into the fabric of their daily operations. Mission and vision statements often failed to manifest in the routine tasks of the workplace.

Nithya Ruff's journey provides valuable insights into company culture, particularly how it can be cultivated and integrated into daily operations. Key takeaways are detailed next.

- **Passion and alignment.** Nithya's passion for learning and her alignment with the technical topics at Amazon exemplify the importance of shared enthusiasm. When employees are genuinely passionate about their work, it contributes to a positive and engaging company culture.

- **Consistency and integration.** At Amazon, Nithya experiences a distinctive and robust culture. The company's leadership principles and operational processes are consistently applied across different sectors. This consistency ensures that the cultural essence remains intact and is deeply embedded in daily practices.

- **Onboarding and reinforcement.** Amazon's meticulous approach involves integrating culture into the onboarding process and reinforcing it at different times of the year. This deliberate effort ensures that employees understand and embody the company's values, fostering a cohesive and aligned workforce.

- **Unique vernacular.** Nithya's mastery of Amazon's unique vernacular is crucial for success, especially in areas like open source.

- **Challenges in other organizations.** Nithya's experience highlights that defining and infusing culture can be challenging in other organizations. Despite mission and vision statements, culture often fails to manifest in day-to-day tasks. Companies should actively bridge this gap to create a thriving work environment.

Amazon was founded by Jeff Bezos in his Bellevue, Washington, garage on July 5, 1994. The company started as an online marketplace for books before expanding to include a range of products, earning the nickname "the everything store." From humble beginnings to being valued at $1.88 trillion in 2023, Amazon truly has come a long way. The key to its success has been astute leadership, but its strong foundation and commitment to the company culture has helped it to stay steadfast to achieve its yearly goals.

Amazon's Key Cultural Norms

Amazon's key cultural norms are listed next.

- **Customer obsession.** Amazon's success is driven by its unwavering focus on customer satisfaction. Employees are encouraged to think from the customer's perspective, innovate, and deliver exceptional experiences. Whether it's improving delivery speed or enhancing product features, customer needs always come first.

- **Ownership and accountability.** Amazon promotes a culture of ownership. Employees are empowered to take initiative, make decisions, and be accountable for outcomes. This entrepreneurial spirit fosters risk taking and drives innovation.

- **Long-term thinking.** Amazon's commitment to long-term goals sets it apart from other technology companies. Instead of pursuing short-term gains, the company invests in innovation, infrastructure, and sustainable growth. This mindset influences everything from product development to employee career paths.

- **Diversity and inclusion.** Amazon values diversity and inclusivity. Affinity groups like the Black Employee Network (BEN), Amazon People With Disabilities (Amazon PWD), and Asians@ Amazon create a supportive environment. The company appreciates different viewpoints and backgrounds.

- **Innovation by working backward.** Amazon's unique approach involves starting with the desired outcome and working backward. Teams write press releases and FAQs before building products, ensuring clarity, alignment, and customer-centric solutions.

- **Agility and adaptability.** Amazon embraces change. Its ability to pivot quickly, experiment, and learn from failures contributes to its agility. Employees are encouraged to adapt, iterate, and stay ahead of market shifts. By adhering to these foundational values, Amazon has achieved significant market and talent success.

Navigating the Unwritten Rules of Company Culture

Navigating a new organization can be challenging. Whether you've been hired as a leader of a new team, of a product, of a business division, or as an individual contributor, you're expected to fulfill your commitments promptly to help the business progress. Failing to meet these expectations can lead to severe consequences, such as losing your job or being placed on a performance improvement plan. Additionally, such failure can damage your reputation and erode trust in the short term. A new hire who fails to recognize the company's emphasis on open communication and chooses to work in isolation may miss valuable feedback and collaborative support, which can lead to lower-quality work, missed deadlines, and a weakened professional reputation within the organization.

Networking helps you learn more about your organization, including how to work effectively with your peers and boss. Networking with others helps you grasp the bigger picture of your organization, meet new people, and learn new ideas while providing insights into what is important for your company. For new hires, networking is especially valuable. By connecting with colleagues across different departments, you can gain a deeper understanding of your role and how it fits into the company's overall strategy. Connecting and building relationships can also help you identify key stakeholders and mentors who can offer guidance and support as you navigate your new job. Additionally, building these relationships can lead to collaborative opportunities, making it easier to integrate into the company culture and contribute meaningfully to your team's goals. Other options to help you network include finding a mentor in your organization, joining an employee resource group or an employee activity group, or volunteering in different programs your organization supports.

Find a Mentor

My parents passed on their love for movies and sci-fi to me. During my formative years, our home housed nearly 200 VHS tapes—a diverse collection ranging from classics like *The Guns of Navarone* and *The Sound of Music* to my personal favorites, *Star Trek* and *Star Wars*. Our family bonding ritual revolved around watching these films, dissecting their themes, and drawing parallels to real-life situations. The magic of cinema became a canvas for our discussions, sparking curiosity and igniting our imaginations. So, it's no wonder my mother used a movie to help me learn an important lesson.

I was 13 years old and dedicated to pursuing my black belt in karate. I had been working toward the belt for several years and had just a year or more to go. Somewhere in this long journey, school and being a teenager distracted me from my goal. My mother noticed this and realized I was pivoting away from a goal I had worked hard to achieve over many years. Instead of giving me a lecture or trying to help me see the path directly, she brought home a VHS cassette of a movie called *Karate Kid*. The movie shares the path of a young boy learning karate from a wise teacher. I was hooked. My mom had to extend the rental of the cassette with our local video rental store because I wanted to rewatch the movie so many times. I loved watching the "wax on, wax off" training session scene. The scene that I am referencing shows the main character, Daniel LaRusso, waxing his teacher's old car. Mr. Miyagi, the teacher, gives the boy seemingly unrelated tasks that help him learn karate, but the boy doesn't understand yet what he's learning. In fact, the young boy is confused as to why he's waxing a car when he initially reached out to Mr. Miyagi to learn how to fight. Originally the boy was looking for fast results. Unknown to him, with each action of adding the wax (wax on) and removing the wax (wax off), he was learning the foundational skills of blocking a punch. This is revealed later in the movie. That was a light bulb moment for me. Thanks to the inspiration from this movie and the support of my parents, I achieved my goal of earning a black belt.

Seeing a mentor/mentee relationship play out in this movie inspired me. Daniel LaRusso's learning and hard work inspired me as did Mr. Miyagi's wisdom and support anytime Daniel thought of giving up his karate lessons. Mr. Miyagi shared life lessons—including techniques that emphasized balance, discipline, and honor—and helped Daniel grow and learn as a result.

In recent years, companies have started buddy programs during onboarding. Research has shown that new hires usually need more help than what their direct manager or team members can provide. They call it a buddy system because they help to find you someone who is in a similar role or area. Although this idea is becoming more popular, not all companies offer such programs. Chances are, you will need to look for a mentor yourself. Mentors should be people you admire and want to learn from. Ideally, they can help you to understand the power dynamics and the way of doing things in your new company.

Types of Mentoring

Mentoring is a valuable process for learning and personal, or career, development, involving a relationship between a mentor and a mentee. Personally, through several years of working in Silicon Valley, I was able to connect and learn from many individuals, which helped me build a network of friends and mentors. I also call them my panel of mentors. Each person offers a different area of expertise. For instance, I might reach out to Mentor A for strategic help and to Mentor B for more specific subject matter expertise. There are also times when I just want another person to understand my situation and give me examples of how they navigated through a tough situation at work. These relationships didn't happen overnight, and the connections didn't even start with mentorship in mind, but you have to hold on to the people who value you, who are ready to give you their time and help guide you. If you invest in this process and continue learning, you can become a mentor and learn from your mentees, too.

Your organization might have different types of opportunities to find mentors internally. Next I discuss different types of mentoring that serve various purposes and goals.

- **One-on-one mentoring** is the traditional form of mentoring, where a mentor and a mentee are paired based on their interests, skills, or goals. They meet regularly to exchange experiences, provide feedback, and offer guidance.
- **Peer mentoring** involves two individuals at a similar stage in their career or life who enter a mentoring relationship. They support each other, share ideas, and learn from each other's challenges and successes.

- **Group mentoring** involves a single mentor working with a group of mentees who have similar needs or objectives. The mentor facilitates group discussions, activities, and learning opportunities, fostering a collaborative learning environment.

- **Reverse mentoring** involves a younger or less experienced person mentoring an older or more experienced individual. The mentor shares insights, perspectives, and skills on topics such as technology, social media, or diversity, providing a fresh viewpoint.

- **Flash mentoring** is a one-time or short-term interaction between a mentor and a mentee to address a specific issue or question. The mentor offers quick advice, feedback, or information to help the mentee with immediate concerns.

- **Team mentoring** consists of a team of mentors working with a team of mentees who are collaborating on a common project or goal. The mentors provide their expertise, guidance, and support to the mentees, either as a group or individually.

- **Virtual mentoring** occurs through online platforms such as email, video chat, or social media. It helps overcome geographical, time, or logistical barriers, allowing mentors and mentees to connect and interact remotely.

- **External mentoring** involves mentors external to your organization, which are very important. Contacts outside your company help you anchor on your strengths that helped you to build your resume externally and give you an external and unbiased perspective. An external mentor can provide you with a more transparent approach when guidance is needed.

Employee Resource Groups

An employee resource group (ERG) is a voluntary assembly of employees who share a common characteristic, interest, or identity with the goal of promoting a more diverse and inclusive workplace culture. ERGs offer support, networking, mentoring, and professional development opportunities for their members while also contributing to the company's overall diversity, equity, and inclusion (DEI) initiatives. Examples of ERGs include groups based on gender, ethnicity, religion, sexual orientation, disability, and lifestyle. These groups help employees feel more connected, valued, and engaged in their work environment.

In 2003, when I started my first job, I was the only person in my department who was an immigrant woman of color. This made no difference to me in my work but, on a regular basis, I was asked questions by team members about my heritage, language, and clothes. Initially I took a lot of pride in answering these questions as I saw this as my way of educating people around me. After some time, though, these questions made me feel that I was different. Although the organization was quite large, I couldn't find people with similar backgrounds who shared my experiences. At times, this frustrated me. As I grew through my career and found my voice, I took it upon myself to start ERGs in my organizations. Doing so was easier in companies where the leadership provided support and much harder where such groups were seen as just another fun employee activity.

In the last decade, companies have started supporting ERGs. When they do, they usually share this information and encourage employees to sign up when they join the company. Doing so is not required or necessary, yet it offers employees a way to join groups of people they can relate to while offering networking and a sense of belonging. You might choose to wait to join an ERG until after you have a handle on your new duties and relationships. In a past job, I spent all my time learning about my role and the company. Initially I didn't have time to spare to join an ERG. I eventually signed up for one when I had time to invest in the group. I considered the ERG an extension of my learning, and belonging to the group helped me to meet several cross-functional leaders earlier than I would have otherwise.

New hires can benefit from joining an ERG in a number of ways, as discussed next.

- **Employee engagement.** As a new hire, joining an ERG can help you quickly find social connections and friends, fostering a sense of belonging in your new workplace.

- **Inclusion.** ERGs provide a safe and supportive environment where you can connect with colleagues who share similar identities or interests. Joining such groups can help you feel more comfortable and empowered to raise awareness and advocate for positive changes.

- **Professional development.** ERGs offer valuable opportunities for networking, mentoring, and skill development. Engaging with these groups can help you learn more about your role, gain new skills, and advance your career.

- **Retention.** Being part of an ERG can enhance your job satisfaction and loyalty, making you feel more valued and engaged.

- **Business innovation.** ERGs contribute to the company's DEI strategy by offering insights into diverse markets and customers. Your involvement can help foster creativity and innovation within the organization.

By participating in an ERG, you can better understand your job, feel more connected to your colleagues, and actively contribute to a positive and inclusive workplace culture.

Here are a few examples of ERGs.

- **Women's network.** A women's network can provide you with support and empowerment in the workplace. Such groups advocate for gender equality and inclusion, helping you navigate your new role with confidence. For example, you might find mentorship opportunities that guide you through your career development.

- **Differently abled networks.** These groups offer a supportive community for employees with disabilities. As a new hire, you can benefit from resources and advocacy that help you integrate smoothly into the workplace. For instance, you might receive assistance in setting up accommodations that enhance your productivity.

- **LGBTQ+ networks.** Joining an LGBTQ+ network can provide a safe and supportive space for you as a new hire. These groups promote awareness and education on LGBTQ+ issues, helping you feel more comfortable and accepted. You might participate in events that foster a sense of community and belonging.

- **Veterans support groups.** If you are a veteran, these groups can help you transition to civilian life and offer resources for career development. As a new hire, you can benefit from mentorship and community service opportunities that align with your background and skills.

- **Sustainability committee.** For new hires passionate about environmental issues, joining a sustainability committee can be highly rewarding. This group fosters environmental awareness and initiates green practices within the organization. You might get involved in projects that promote sustainability and corporate responsibility.

- **Young professionals network.** Joining a young professionals network can help early-career employees connect with peers and mentors. Such groups organize social and professional events that enhance your skills and expand your network. For example, you might attend workshops that improve your job performance and career prospects.

Explore Company Volunteer Programs

In 2013 when I joined Salesforce, the company had fewer than 10,000 employees. On the first day of group orientation, we received a half-day agenda on the topics to be covered. We were asked to keep the second half of the day clear and open. I was excited, to say the least. Salesforce was an up-and-coming company with great profits, an excellent market product, and a fiercely competitive leader. The day started well with the usual welcome sessions from a few business leaders, who shared the history of the company and the big vision and goals. Over the course of the day, we introduced ourselves. I felt happy to be in a room full of people who came from different industries and experiences.

Something happened toward the end of the first half of the day that changed my perspective about the company and my role as an employee. The head of their foundation (community giving) arrived to talk about the work Salesforce does with its communities. Until then, I had heard of only a few companies that focused their efforts in supporting their communities. I thought they did this by donating money. The head of the foundation shared how the foundation started and the impact its work made. I was thrilled to hear about this and wrote notes in my orientation workbook (like a graduate student), thinking there might be a test at the end of the session. But they surprised me by asking us to go into the community right then to work with a few of the nongovernmental organizations for the afternoon.

> When you work together as a team for a selfless purpose, the bond you create is strong.

My previous company experiences had been all about the business side. Here we were about to roll up our sleeves to give back to the community on the very first day of becoming an employee. This experience helped our cohort get to know each other better. When you work together as a team for a selfless purpose, the bond you create is strong. I am still friends with many of those cohort members because we shared a common purpose beyond ourselves.

My first day at Salesforce was one of the most memorable and rewarding experiences I've had. I left that evening feeling both fulfilled and energized, and the sense of belonging didn't end there—it became an ongoing commitment for new hires every year. Volunteering allowed me to connect with the company's mission, build relationships, and learn from my peers in a meaningful way. Most large organizations have foundation or community extension opportunities available. If your company does, you should sign up for them. You can ask your human resources team about such opportunities, check on your company website, or work with your hiring manager to plan the best way for you to volunteer. Companies also offer "matching" as a way to encourage employees to give back to the community. For instance, if you raise $1,000 for a charity or nongovernmental organization you want to serve, your company might match that amount. Other ways of giving back to the community include teaching STEM topics in schools, doing team events to build homes or support food packaging, and sharing your expertise on certain products like Excel for free with government or public organizations.

As you step into a new role, embracing corporate volunteer programs can significantly benefit you and your team. Engaging in meaningful volunteer work can boost productivity, as it often translates to increased motivation and focus in professional roles. Volunteering provides employees with a sense of purpose and connection to their community, leading to enhanced engagement with their work and the organization. Engaged employees tend to be more committed, productive, and satisfied. Volunteering will give you a sense of purpose beyond your daily work tasks, allowing you to contribute to causes you care about and fostering a deeper connection to your work and the organization. Most important, volunteering provides opportunities for networking and relationship building, as it often involves collaborating with others both within and outside the company.

The numerous volunteering opportunities can engage those with a variety of skills and interests. If the examples provided don't resonate with your passion, check with your HR team about volunteer time or donation matching programs, as policies differ by company. In terms of specific activities, you can contribute to the environment by engaging in reforestation, beach cleanups, or nature trail construction or by managing invasive species. For animal lovers, volunteering at shelters, sanctuaries, wildlife centers, or zoos offers opportunities to walk dogs, pet cats, clean cages, or answer phones. Social volunteering includes working at soup kitchens, food banks, homeless shelters, senior centers, or schools as well as mentoring, tutoring, coaching, or fundraising for various causes. In the healthcare sector, volunteers can assist at hospitals, clinics, nursing homes, or hospices, providing emotional support, companionship, or information to patients and their families.

For those passionate about sports and leisure, opportunities exist to volunteer at events, clubs, or organizations, where you can teach, coach, referee, or cheer. Additionally, tech companies often partner with local schools and colleges for STEM teaching opportunities at various levels, allowing employees to share their expertise. By exploring these options, you can find a volunteering activity that aligns with your interests and skills, enabling you to make a meaningful impact in your community.

Strategic Participation

With so many choices in your new company, chances are you might feel too overwhelmed to participate in activities or feel confused on how to best balance your time as you are learning and orienting yourself to your surroundings. I faced this problem when I joined Google because I had heard so much about their perks and activities that I wanted to be part of it all. I was newly married and had recently moved to a new city, and I was eager to make friends. As I reflect on my time there, I think I overindexed on participation to fit in and didn't do enough to focus on my learning and productivity.

Over the years of taking on new roles and growing in my career, I have come to recognize that since you have limited time and energy in a day, you need to plan it very well. Strategic participation will help you to invest in those areas where you can get the maximum out of your contribution.

When you sign up for employee events in your company, ask yourself why you are participating. Are you participating to network, learn, give to a cause, or something else? Some events can also be useful for getting visibility or access to your executive leaders. For instance, in one of my previous companies, we used to have a Thanksgiving lunch that was attended by almost 100% of the employees because executive leaders served the food. Employees saw this as a significant opportunity to connect with their executive team and gain valuable insights. Prioritizing activities like this can deepen your understanding of company culture and leadership, but balancing them with work demands is essential. If pressing deadlines take precedence, skipping a lunch-and-learn session may be the wiser choice unless it contributes to productivity or meaningful networking.

Career Pointers

1. Consider why you care about learning a new company's culture. How will doing so help you?

2. Go through the steps to identify and find the ideal culture for you.

3. Note what is most important to you in a company's culture.

4. You'll find a variety of company cultures exist. Review the examples in this strategy to gain a deeper understanding of differences. Doing so can be especially helpful if you're still trying to figure out what will serve you best.

5. Use the steps in this strategy to find a mentor who can help you acclimate to the culture, and consider ways you can help them, too.

6. If your company offers employee resource groups, find out what's offered and determine if you want to join one.

7. If your company offers volunteer opportunities, learn more about what types are offered and decide if any appeal to you.

Keep Learning

Be passionate and bold. Always keep learning. You stop doing useful things if you don't learn.

—Satya Nadella

A **FEW YEARS AGO,** during a one-on-one meeting with my then direct reporting leader, I was introduced to a transformative idea that shifted my perspective. Fresh from a conference where discussions revolved around the power of growth mindsets, my leader shared insights on their potential to enhance individual learning and influence organizational trajectories the concept was called growth mindset.

Despite my usual diligence in staying updated on the latest research in my field, I found myself momentarily at a loss. It was one of those rare occasions where I felt embarrassed by my lack of understanding. I paused, gathered my thoughts, and mustered the courage to inquire about the concept's essence. My leader met my query with a reassuring smile, acknowledging my willingness to learn by saying "Shveta, your question demonstrates a growth mindset—a willingness to embrace new knowledge and ideas."

Embracing a philosophy of lifelong learning has been my guiding principle and source of strength. However, it wasn't until that conversation that I delved into the compelling evidence from social psychology, which highlights the importance of continual learning across all stages of life. This discussion ignited my deep exploration into the concept, an exploration that led us to integrate it into the fabric of our organizational culture. From defining its significance to embodying it through our actions and encouraging its adoption among new hires, employees, and company leaders, we made a concerted effort to instill a culture of continuous learning.

Coinciding with the festive holiday season in December, our commitment was further bolstered by gifting copies of Carol Dweck's seminal work, *Mindset: The New Psychology of Success* (2007), to the senior leadership team—an invaluable resource that complemented our journey toward fostering a growth-oriented mindset within our organization. In his 2019 book *Hit Refresh*, Satya Nadella, CEO of Microsoft, talks about his exploration of a growth mindset in his work and role as the CEO.

Nadella shares how he has made the growth mindset the focus of his life, which in turn has helped him to turn around Microsoft. He has been instrumental in Microsoft's resurgence as a tech titan. He steered the company toward cloud computing and artificial intelligence, leading to a decade of remarkable growth and a cultural shift that emphasizes innovation and customer-centricity. Under his leadership, Microsoft's market valuation skyrocketed, outperforming the S&P 500 with a more than tenfold increase in stock value. Nadella's strategic acquisitions and expansion of cross-platform services, including bringing Microsoft Office to mobile platforms, have solidified Microsoft's position in the tech industry. His tenure has not only rejuvenated Microsoft but also established it as a formidable competitor in the global market, with its valuation briefly touching $3 trillion.

Growth Mindset versus Fixed Mindset in Your New Role

Early in my career, I moved from a specialist role to a manager role with a small team of four quite rapidly. Having a team that helped me to scale my programs was helpful yet also meant I had to learn a few new things as I made the transition from a specialist to a people leader. My job at that time was to build elearning content for training purposes for company employees. I had a certain way of editing and writing my content, which had worked for me for several years. However, when I took on the team, they had interesting ways of doing the same work that made it faster to deliver the training. At first, I assumed my way was the right way. This is an example of having a fixed mindset. I was being a know-it-all, and this attitude slowed down my team. We didn't keep up with the latest editing and publishing technologies, and I could see we were not doing well. The motivation of the team was also at its lowest point. Through some reflection and support of my team, I was able to learn, get up to speed, and enable my team to move fast to deliver stronger results. I eventually moved to a growth mindset. If I had had that mindset early on, the success of my team and my work would have been faster and with fewer bumps in the road.

In a *Forbes* Council Post from 2021, Rajal C., founder and CEO of Gravitas, writes:

> *A fixed mindset creates an internal monologue (self-talk) that is focused on judging the emotions, behaviors and actions of ourselves and others. On the opposite end of the spectrum, people with a growth mindset are also constantly monitoring what's going on, but their internal monologue is not about judging themselves and others in this way.*

For a new hire, embracing a growth mindset is crucial as it fosters resilience, encourages learning from feedback and mistakes, and promotes adaptability in the face of challenges. It enables individuals to view obstacles as opportunities for growth, leading to continuous personal and professional development. This mindset is particularly valuable in today's work environments, where the ability to learn and evolve is key to long-term success.

Why Is Continuous Learning Important?

In the spring of 2024, a long-awaited family excursion to Italy materialized. For three years, circumstances thwarted our plans, but the anticipation only fueled my meticulous preparation. I charted our journey across Italian cities with precision, down to hourly itineraries. The trip promised a wealth of knowledge and an abundance of steps—indeed, a month's quota of walking condensed into seven days.

The Sistine Chapel held a special allure. I first heard about the chapel during a sixth-grade history lesson in India, where it was lauded as a Renaissance masterpiece. As my textbook lacked pictures, the chapel remained an abstract concept until I saw it in person and stood inside its walls. The sight of Michelangelo's *Last Judgment* was arresting; the gallery's hush deepened into reverence as a prayer echoed. Our guide's narrative of Michelangelo's artistic odyssey added layers to the visual splendor.

Michelangelo's legacy extends beyond his masterpieces; it is deeply rooted in his relentless pursuit of knowledge. His mastery of the fresco technique—an emblem of artistic excellence—was not merely an achievement but a testament to his unwavering dedication to skill and precision. His dedication to honing new skills was evident as he painstakingly adorned the Sistine Chapel's ceiling—a testament to hard work and an insatiable quest for knowledge. This four-year endeavor, from 1508 to 1512, stands as a monument to his lifelong commitment to learning.

His maxim, "I am still learning," encapsulates his enduring pursuit of growth and knowledge. It's a philosophy that resonates deeply, emphasizing the value of continuous learning over mere tenure.

As I meandered through Rome, reflecting on the Sistine Chapel and Michelangelo's devotion to lifelong learning, it struck me that true success is not tethered to years of experience but to an unwavering dedication to continual self-improvement. Understanding this can help you as you start your new role. Consider the business significance of lifelong learning.

Companies that emphasize ongoing education are better equipped to navigate the evolving market and industry shifts. They focus on nurturing their current workforce, which fosters internal talent development over exclusive dependence on new recruitment and training.

Regarding personal advancement for the workforce, a commitment to continuous learning equates to enduring advancement in both personal and professional lives. Although seminars and symposiums offer substantial insights, it's the reinforcement through persistent learning that guarantees a profound and permanent influence.

It's essential to recognize that continuous learning transcends a singular occurrence; it embodies a philosophy that cultivates perpetual progress and versatility within both the individual and the corporate entity.

Types of Continuous Learning

Continuous learning is the practice of expanding one's skills and knowledge as part of an ongoing process of self-improvement or professional development. It involves actively seeking out learning opportunities beyond formal education or initial training.

Formal learning or structured learning is characterized by organized instructional sessions led by educators, either in person or online. Organizations frequently provide these educational programs to acclimate new employees, impart specific competencies, or groom individuals for leadership positions.

Social learning is an informal approach that occurs naturally as employees engage with their work environment and interact with peers. Social learning encompasses collaborative learning with colleagues, guidance under mentorship programs, and experiential learning through job shadowing, enabling the assimilation of hands-on skills and valuable insights. Julie Sweet, at the helm of Accenture, champions the ethos of perpetual learning and self-improvement. She often discusses "learning agility" as a pivotal skill, emphasizing the need to be nimble and adaptable in acquiring new knowledge. In her personal and professional life, Sweet embodies this principle by regularly interacting with thought leaders across different sectors, ensuring she remains at the forefront of innovation.

Self-directed learning involves individuals taking the initiative to pursue knowledge independently. It may involve engaging with digital media such as podcasts and TED Talks, reading articles, or investigating specialized subjects. Self-directed learning is particularly beneficial for honing specialized skills or navigating transitions in one's career trajectory.

A Checklist for Your First Three Months

On joining your new organization, you will probably need to go through several new training sessions (online and some in person) during your orientation process. In my two decades of working in different technology companies, every single one of them had several hours of training designed for new hires. In some cases, these training courses started before the first day and would include information about the company culture and company benefits. These courses are usually aimed to get new hires excited about their new role.

Crafting an effective learning strategy is a good way to focus on your learning and manage your time effectively. These strategies will help you plan effectively and enhance your learning efficiency.

Boost Your Memory

- Engage in regular exercise, get plenty of sleep, and interact socially to improve memory.
- Minimize distractions and structure your study material for better memorization.
- Employ visual aids and verbal repetition to strengthen retention.

Embrace Continuous Learning

- Keep your brain active by consistently learning new things.
- The brain is capable of generating new cells through neurogenesis, and active learning helps sustain the new cells.

Diversify Your Learning Methods

- Use a mix of reading, auditory learning, discussions, and practical exercises.
- Teaching others what you've learned can deepen your own understanding.

Link New Ideas to Known Concepts

- Connect fresh information to your existing knowledge base to help remember and apply it in various situations.

Get Hands-on

- Look for practical applications of your knowledge through experiments or projects, which can solidify your learning.

Learn from Your Errors

- Recognize that making mistakes is a natural part of the learning curve.

- Reflect on these errors, make adjustments, and use them as growth opportunities.

Stay Consistent

- Opt for daily study habits over last-minute cramming to better integrate and retain information.

Self-Evaluate

- Regular self-testing can help cement knowledge and pinpoint areas needing improvement.

Single-Task Focus

- Avoid juggling tasks. Concentrate on one subject at a time to improve focus and understanding.

Be Accountable

- Set clear learning goals, establish a study routine, and monitor your progress to maintain motivation and consistency.

A well-crafted learning plan, or personal learning syllabus, can be an invaluable asset for anyone aiming to achieve specific educational goals, whether you're a student, a working professional, or simply on a quest for personal development. It serves as a structured guide to navigate your educational pursuits efficiently.

Becoming 37% Better

In *Atomic Habits* (2018), author James Clear emphasizes the profound impact of making small, incremental changes—improving just 1% every day. He suggests that these tiny improvements can be surprisingly powerful in the long run, potentially leading to being 37 times better over the course of a year.

Clear advises shifting focus from setting goals to designing systems that facilitate these small changes. He argues that goals are about the results you want to achieve while systems are the processes that lead to those results. If you're struggling to change your habits, it's not a personal failure but a failure of the system in place. These ideas from James Clear can help you focus on making small changes to your "system" as you continue to learn and grow your skill sets.

Refining Skills over Time

Adopting a growth mindset—believing that skills can be developed through dedication—can significantly enhance your ability to learn. Mastery is an ongoing journey, and regular practice is essential for sharpening abilities. Knowing your learning preferences, whether you're a visual, auditory, or kinesthetic learner, can make acquiring new skills more efficient. Access to various resources, such as books, online courses, and mentors, greatly influences your learning experience, especially with the abundance of information available in the digital age. Being open to constructive feedback from colleagues or mentors can accelerate your improvement. Last, embracing a commitment to lifelong learning is vital.

As Steve Jobs famously suggested, there's always something new to discover. Cultivating curiosity and remaining open to new knowledge is crucial for continuous personal and professional growth.

Continuous learning is the fuel that powers my creative thinking and innovative problem-solving abilities, contributing significantly to my personal development and positioning me as a leader who can embrace the future. Staying abreast of new technologies and market trends helps me maintain relevance and flexibility in my role. Being in an organization that champions learning cultivates my curiosity and proactivity, enhancing my performance and job satisfaction. I place a high value on career progression and skill enhancement, viewing them as more important than mere financial gain, and I see continuous learning as the key to unlocking these aspirations. Ensuring my skills are up-to-date is vital for my professional success and personal satisfaction. Moreover, a culture that prioritizes learning offers me the chance to evolve within my company, presenting new challenges and opportunities for growth without the need to seek them elsewhere. For me, continuous learning isn't just a concept; it's the cornerstone of a proactive, growth-oriented mindset that prepares me for the future and allows me to actively shape it.

Kobe Bryant, the legendary basketball player, exemplified continuous learning at the peak of his career. Known for his relentless work ethic and dedication to improvement, Bryant's daily routine was a testament to his commitment to excellence. Even after winning multiple NBA championships and earning the respect of the basketball world, he never became complacent. Bryant often arrived at the gym before dawn to practice, spending hours on his shooting, footwork, and conditioning. He worked closely with his coaches to refine his skills and sought feedback from his peers to understand different perspectives.

Bryant's dedication to continuous learning was not limited to his physical abilities. He studied game films exhaustively to gain a mental edge over his opponents. He believed that understanding the game deeply was just as important as physical training. This approach helped him adapt and evolve his game over his career, allowing him to remain a dominant force in the NBA for years. His story serves as a powerful example of how even the most talented individuals can benefit from a mindset of lifelong learning and daily practice. His legacy is not just one of talent but of an unyielding pursuit of growth and mastery, making him an ideal role model for anyone looking to excel in their field.

Your Well-Being

In the early stages of my HR career, I sought guidance from a seasoned colleague who had a wealth of experience. Her journey began in a technical role, transitioned into finance as a financial analyst, and culminated in her leading the talent division within the same company for over two decades. Our routine catch-ups, which occurred multiple times each quarter, were rich with exchanges of insights, project updates, and personal connections. On one such occasion, she perceived a dip in my usual vivacity and inquired about my well-being. My response was a halfhearted chuckle, followed by a quip about the luxury of self-care in our fast-paced environment. She empathized by recounting a challenging episode from her past: a presentation to a group of engineering managers that went awry, pushing her to the brink of tears. That evening, as fate would have it, she tuned into a podcast on self-care and resilience. It sparked a moment of self-reflection, leading her to affirm the importance of acknowledging even the smallest victories, like persevering through a tough presentation—a modest triumph yet a significant stride in her journey.

She realized that self-compassion was not just a personal indulgence but a professional necessity. From that day on, she made a conscious effort to celebrate her achievements no matter how small. She started a journal, documenting moments of resilience and instances where she overcame adversity. This practice bolstered her confidence and served as a reminder of her growth.

She shared this newfound perspective with me, emphasizing the power of recognizing our own strengths and the courage it takes to face challenges head-on. Her words resonated deeply, prompting me to reevaluate my own approach to self-care and resilience. I began to see that taking care of oneself isn't a detour from the path to success. Instead, selfcare is the very pavement that supports the journey. I started noticing better levels of energy that not only made me more productive at work but helped me to spend quality time with my family.

This lesson became a cornerstone of my professional journey. As someone who led enterprise strategy for the past two decades in Fortune 500 companies, I advocated for a culture that honors self-care and resilience as pillars of professional development. These values need to be integrated during onboarding programs because they support new employees in their roles and empower them to thrive amid the complexities of corporate life.

Feeling stress when starting a new professional journey is normal. However, by employing a set of thoughtful strategies, you can effectively navigate this stress and place a strong emphasis on your personal well-being as you transition into your new position. It's important to recognize that this period of adjustment is a learning curve—a time rich with opportunities for growth and self-discovery.

As you integrate into your new environment, remember:

- **Flexibility.** Be adaptable and open to new methods and ideas, which can reduce stress and lead to innovative problem-solving.

- **Patience.** Allow yourself the grace to learn at your own pace. Patience is a virtue that will serve you well in times of change.

- **Self-care.** Prioritize activities that nurture your mind, body, and spirit. Whether it's exercise, meditation, or a hobby, self-care is crucial.

- **Ask for help.** Don't shy away from leaning on friends, family, or professionals for support when you need it.

- **Acknowledge and celebrate your wins.** Doing this can boost your confidence and motivation.

By focusing on these additional aspects, you'll not only manage stress but also enhance your overall job satisfaction and performance. Your well-being is a vital component of your professional success; never underestimate its power. As you continue on this path, let your well-being be the guiding light that leads you to fulfillment and achievement in your new role.

Managing your well-being is not just part of our corporate jobs. We see this every day in different fields, especially in the life of athletes. Simone Biles, the renowned gymnast from the United States, stands out as an athlete who gives top priority to her personal well-being to stay at the top of her game. Her bold move to step back from multiple events at the Tokyo Olympics to concentrate on her mental health sent ripples across the sports world, earning acclaim for underscoring the significance of an athlete's well-being. Biles hasn't shied away from discussing the heavy burdens that come with competitive sports and the critical role mental health plays for athletes. Her candidness sparked wider discussions on the intense mental and emotional pressures elite athletes face and the importance of having supportive structures in place for their well-being. By choosing to prioritize her mental health, Biles highlighted the vital importance of self-care as a key component in reaching and maintaining elite athletic performance levels.

Well-being is a topic of focus in the corporate world, too. Arianna Huffington, the visionary behind *The Huffington Post* and Thrive Global, a well-being and behavior change platform, had an epiphany after burning out from overwork. This led her to become a staunch proponent of the idea that well-being is crucial for peak productivity and performance. In her writings, including her books *The Sleep Revolution* (Huffington 2017) and *Thrive* (Huffington 2014), Huffington champions the essential nature of rest and recuperation in the pursuit of professional excellence. She makes the case that well-being and productivity go hand in hand, suggesting that a focus on personal health can enhance decision making, unleash creativity, and elevate work results.

As a leader, Huffington practices what she preaches by urging her team to prioritize self-care, step away from the digital world, and engage in restorative activities. She's convinced that when people are mentally and physically refreshed, they're not just more productive; they're also more effective contributors to their organizations. In the realm of business leadership, well-being is increasingly becoming a strategic priority. Take Satya Nadella, Microsoft's CEO, for instance. He's reshaped the company's ethos, focusing on empathy and fostering a culture of continuous growth. Then there's Marc Benioff, the cofounder and CEO of Salesforce, who's a big advocate for mindfulness, weaving it into the very fabric of his company's values.

Robin Chase, the entrepreneurial force behind Zipcar and now at the helm of Tucows, finds her equilibrium in the tranquility of gardening and the rhythmic flow of knitting. Doug Zingale of Blue Goose Capital ensures his well-being by carving out time for family, regular workouts, and even weekly massages despite his bustling schedule.

These trailblazers recognize that managing stress and nurturing a balanced lifestyle sets a sterling example for their teams while enhancing their health. They're proponents of practices like meditation and physical exercise, and they understand the importance of disconnecting to maintain mental and physical sharpness. Their commitment to well-being is a testament to its integral role in cultivating effective and sustainable leadership.

The Best-Laid Plans

The phrase "the best-laid plans" comes from Robert Burns's 1785 poem "To a Mouse," which explores themes of human ambition, fate, and the unpredictability of life. Burns wrote the poem after accidentally disturbing a mouse's nest while plowing his field, an experience that led him to reflect on the shared struggles of both humans and animals.

In the poem, Burns expresses sympathy for the mouse, recognizing that despite its careful preparation, an unexpected event—a destroyed nest—has left it vulnerable to the cold winter ahead. He draws a parallel between the mouse's plight and human aspirations, acknowledging that no matter how meticulously one plans, external forces can upend even the most carefully laid groundwork.

Here's an excerpt from the poem:

> *The best-laid schemes o' mice an' men*
> *Gang aft agley,*
> *An' lea'e us nought but grief an' pain,*
> *For promis'd joy!*

Translated, this means that even the most carefully laid plans can go awry, leaving us with disappointment and heartache instead of the anticipated joy. Applying this wisdom to our lives, it's essential to recognize that change is inevitable. No matter how meticulously we plan, external factors—such as shifts in the economy, unexpected health issues, or global events like the COVID-19 pandemic—can disrupt our path. Resilience, adaptability, and a willingness to adjust our plans are necessary.

Life rarely unfolds exactly as we envision it. Embrace the twists and turns, learn from setbacks, and remain open to possibilities. After all, it's often in unplanned moments that we discover our true strength and resilience.

From Starfleet to Your Desk: Take on Challenges the *Star Trek* Way

I mentioned earlier in this book that I am an avid fan of sci-fi movies and series. I was barely 10 years old when I got hooked on *Star Trek*. I always thought it was way ahead of its time in introducing concepts, ideas, and innovative technology. Watching this TV show is where I first learned about the concept of Kobayashi Maru, which symbolizes a scenario where victory is unattainable, serving as a test of one's character when faced with certain defeat. Starfleet Academy uses the concept to challenge cadets with a rescue mission doomed to fail, assessing their decision making, leadership, and ethics under duress.

Although Kobayashi Maru is a fantasy concept from the movie *Star Trek II: The Wrath of Khan*, you can utilize this idea in your new role. When starting a new job, think of the Kobayashi Maru as an analogy for those daunting tasks where success is uncertain or the best course of action is murky. Here's how to leverage this idea in your new position:

- **Confront challenges.** Recognize that not all situations have a straightforward route to triumph. Embracing this reality allows you to concentrate on aspects within your power.

- **Use creative problem solving.** Be inspired by Captain Kirk's approach. He says, "I don't believe in the no-win scenario." To alter the simulation for a win, seek inventive ways to redefine the problem's boundaries.

- **Make principled choices.** The exercise compels you to balance the potential sacrifices against the gains, sharpening your capacity for difficult moral decisions.

- **Steer through stress.** The concept gauges your ability to steer and stay poised during critical decisions, an essential trait for any new role.

- **Grow through setbacks.** Kobayashi Maru is intentionally designed for failure. Each setback is an opportunity for learning, equipping you for high-stakes, real-world challenges.

Embracing the teachings of the Kobayashi Maru equips you to manage the intricacies and pressures of a new job, turning each obstacle into a moment for personal and professional development. Focus on evolving, adapting, and mastering the art of steering through difficult circumstances instead of seeking to conquer every challenge.

Another way to mitigate setbacks is to plan very well. To highlight the importance of planning, let's discuss the race to conquer the South Pole. In 1910, two intrepid explorers, Roald Amundsen and Robert Falcon Scott, set out on separate expeditions to reach the South Pole. Their contrasting approaches and unwavering determination would define their legacies.

Roald Amundsen: The Norwegian Explorer

Roald Amundsen, a seasoned Norwegian explorer, spent much of his life pushing the boundaries of human exploration. His résumé included a voyage to Antarctica in the late 19th century and being the first person to navigate the treacherous Northwest Passage. Amundsen's meticulous planning and thirst for adventure set him apart. His strategy was methodical. He assembled a team of expert dog-sled drivers and skilled skiers. Amundsen's ship, the *Fram*, was anchored on the Ross Ice Shelf and strategically positioned over 60 miles closer to the Pole than Scott's base in McMurdo Sound. Amundsen's singular goal was clear: to be the first to reach the South Pole.

Robert Falcon Scott: British Determination

Robert Falcon Scott, a Royal Navy officer, had led an Antarctic mission in 1902. When his ship, the *Terra Nova*, arrived at Ross Island, Scott's 34-man team focused on scientific research and sample collection. But Scott was determined to claim the Pole for the British Empire. His mission gained urgency when he learned that Amundsen was vying for the same honor.

Amundsen set off on October 20, 1910, relying on expert dog teams and skilled skiers. Scott's journey began on November 1, 1910, with sledges and ponies. The two expeditions followed different paths, but Amundsen's camp was closer to the Pole. On December 14, 1911, Amundsen's team planted the Norwegian flag at the South Pole a full 33 days before Scott and his team arrived.

Tragically, Scott's party was unprepared for the extreme conditions, frostbite, and exhaustion they faced. One of Scott's diary entries read: "Our chance still holds good if we can put the work in, but it's a terribly trying time." But it was too late. Amundsen's meticulous preparation, reliance on dogs, head start, and strategic positioning secured his victory. His lifelong dedication paid off, making him the first person to reach the South Pole. While Scott's determination was admirable, his reliance on ponies and motor sledges proved less effective. His fate serves as a poignant reminder of the challenges of polar exploration. Roald Amundsen's name remains forever linked to the South Pole, while Scott's legacy endures as a testament to human resilience in the face of adversity.

Stepping into a new role brings inevitable shifts—whether it's a change in leadership, a company restructuring, or unpredictable market dynamics. While some of these transitions will be beyond your control, embracing adaptability can help you navigate them with confidence. If you have a well-planned road ahead of you, you will be able to encounter the changes and still be successful.

Your Success Starts with You

As you step into your new role, you'll encounter various shifts— some expected, others unforeseen. External factors can significantly impact your experience. Even though situations might change or not go as expected, your success will depend on your planning, resilience, and ability to navigate through change.

A few years back, I found myself mentoring a new hire who radiated enthusiasm. She was eager to contribute to the organization's goals, but frustration soon crept in. Within her first month, her team underwent a leadership change, and the scope of her role shifted. As a product engineer, the very product she was hired to lead was reassigned to another team lead. Determined to support her, I delved into resources that could provide guidance. That's when I stumbled upon *Ganbatte: The Japanese Art of Always Moving Forward* (2021) by Albert Liebermann. The term "ganbatte" (pronounced gan-ba-tay) is a Japanese philosophy that centers around giving your utmost effort with the resources available to you. Although there isn't a direct English equivalent, the essence of *ganbatte* can be summarized as "keep going" or "give it your all." This mindset embodies resilience, determination, and the unwavering commitment to progress, even when faced with challenges. The principles of *ganbatte* capture the essence of resilience and determination for someone starting a new job.

> External factors can significantly impact your experience. Even though situations might change or not go as expected, your success will depend on your planning, resilience, and ability to navigate through change.

In addition to resilience, you'll need a way to handle the overwhelm. As you are organizing your first 90 days, reviewing information, meeting new people, and learning about the company, you are going to feel overwhelmed. You will need a better way to plan your days and to help prioritize the work that needs to get done. In *A Minute to Think: Reclaim Creativity, Conquer Busyness, and Do Your Best Work* (Funt 2021), Juliet Funt introduces several practical techniques for enhancing productivity and doing your best work. She highlights the critical need for intentional breaks, which she refers to as whitespace, to enhance one's creativity, efficiency, and overall health amid the hustle of our modern lives. Funt shares actionable advice and strategies to empower individuals to master their hectic timetables and provides insights on resisting the prevalent obsession with being constantly busy.

Implementing the concept of whitespace can be extremely helpful for individuals starting a new career. By using whitespace, you can:

- **Mitigate information overload.** The transition to a new role is often accompanied by a deluge of data and duties. Deliberate pauses, or whitespace, enable newcomers to digest information, organize their priorities, and sidestep the potential for overwhelm.

- **Foster knowledge acquisition.** These purposeful intervals are conducive to more effective assimilation and memory of fresh information, which is vital for understanding a new organization's operations and ethos.

- **Sharpen concentration.** Intervals of rest are instrumental in preserving concentration and alertness, which are key for acquiring new competencies and grasping work-related obligations.

- **Elevate job performance.** Evidence suggests that periodic rest can enhance job execution, aiding novices in making a positive and lasting initial impact.

Consider the contrasting approaches of Roald Amundsen and Robert Falcon Scott. Amundsen meticulously planned his South Pole expedition, relying on dogs and strategic positioning. Scott, while determined, faced setbacks due to inadequate preparation that included a lack of focused attention on resilience and not testing things out before launching. The lesson? A well-prepared road map can make all the difference.

Go Get Them, Tiger!

Let me end by sharing something that I hope encourages you. I was enrolled in a new school in a new city in fourth grade. I dreaded taking the new school bus. As I waited in line with my dad, I was chatting away nonstop, something I do when I am nervous. He noticed that and listened to all my stories. When I paused, he squeezed my hand. I looked up to him and he said, "I know you are excited about making new friends and enjoying the school year. Keep up with your energy, and *go get them, tiger!*" I gave him a big hug, and I knew I was going to do my best and learn.

With anything new that happens in my life, his words encourage me to do my best. Your energy and excitement for making an impact in your new job will make you successful. To fuel your success, take charge by building a strong road map.

Career Pointers

1. What types of learning do you want to continue to engage in once you start your new role? What learning will prepare you well for the present and the future?

2. Add whitespace (deliberate pauses) to your day.

3. Map out success for your first 30 days.

4. Talk with your boss about expectations, and be sure to include those goals in your 30-day plan.

Bibliography

Alexis, Michael. 2024, April 8. "18 Strong Work Culture Examples." Team-building. https://teambuilding.com/blog/work-culture-examples.

Amabile, Teresa M., and Steven J. Kramer. 2011, May. "The Power of Small Wins." *Harvard Business Review.* https://hbr.org/2011/05/the-power-of-small-wins.

Amazon Staff. 2024a, August 15. "Our Upskilling 2025 Programs." About Amazon. https://www.aboutamazon.com/news/workplace/our-upskilling-2025-programs.

Amazon Staff. 2024b, September 4. "Amazon's Career Choice Education Benefit for Hourly Employees." https://www.aboutamazon.com/news/workplace/amazon-career-choice-education-benefit.

Amazon Staff. 2024c, August 29. "Amazon Recruiters Share What Successful Job Candidates Do." https://www.aboutamazon.com/news/workplace/successful-amazon-job-candidates.

Avildsen, J. G., dir. 1984. *Karate Kid.* Columbia Pictures.

Baumgartner, Natalie. 2020, April 8. "Build a Culture That Aligns with People's Values." *Harvard Business Review.* https://hbr.org/2020/04/build-a-culture-that-aligns-with-peoples-values.

Bock, Laszlo. 2015. *Work Rules! Insights from Inside Google That Will Transform How You Live and Lead.* New York: Twelve Books.

Carter, Chris. n.d. *Review of X-Files.* Fox.

Chhaya, Nihar. 2022, August 29. "How to Figure Out the Power Dynamics in a New Job." *Harvard Business Review.* https://hbr.org/2022/08/how-to-figure-out-the-power-dynamics-in-a-new-job.

Church, Allan H., and Jay A. Conger. 2018, June 28. "When You Start a New Job, Pay Attention to These 5 Aspects of Company Culture." *Harvard Business Review.* https://hbr.org/2018/03/when-you-start-a-new-job-pay-attention-to-these-5-aspects-of-company-culture.

Clear, James. 2018. *Atomic Habits.* New York: Avery.

Covey, Stephen R., and Rebecca R. Merrill. 2006. *The Speed of Trust: The One Thing That Changes Everything.* New York: Free Press.

Daimler, M. (2022). *RE-CULTURING: Rethink Your Culture to Connect Strategy and Purpose for Lasting Success.* New York: McGraw-Hill.

Development Dimensions International (DDI). n.d.

Drucker, Peter. 2006. *The Practice of Management.* New York: Harper Business.

Dweck, Carol S. 2007. *Mindset: The New Psychology of Success.* New York: Ballantine Books.

Effron, Marc. 2018, November 30. "A Simple Way to Map Out Your Career Ambitions." *Harvard Business Review.* https://hbr.org/2018/11/a-simple-way-to-map-out-your-career-ambitions.

Funt, Juliet. 2021. *A Minute to Think: Reclaim Creativity, Conquer Busyness, and Do Your Best Work.* New York: Harper Business.

van Gennep, Arnold. 1909/1981. *Les Rites de Passage.* Reprint. Paris: A. et J. Picard.

Grove, Andrew S. 2015. *High Output Management.* New York: Vintage.

Groysberg, Boris, Jeremiah Lee, Jesse Price, and J. Yo-Jud Cheng. 2018, January–February. "The Leader's Guide to Corporate Culture." *Harvard Business Review.* https://hbr.org/2018/01/the-leaders-guide-to-corporate-culture.

Haan, Katherine. 2023, June 12. "Top Remote Work Statistics and Trends in 2024." *Forbes.* https://www.forbes.com/advisor/business/remote-work-statistics/.

Huffington, A. 2014. *Thrive: The Third Metric to Redefining Success and Creating a Life of Well-Being, Wisdom, and Wonder.* New York: Harmony.

Huffington, A. 2017. *The Sleep Revolution: Transforming Your Life, One Night at a Time.* New York: Harmony.

Janson, Kimberly. 2022, August 16. "How Authentic Should You Be in the Workplace?" *Forbes Coaches Council Post*. https://www.forbes.com/councils/forbescoachescouncil/2022/08/16/how-authentic-should-you-be-in-the-workplace/.

Krattenmaker, Tom. 2000. "What's Your Company's Culture?" Harvard Business Publishing Education. https://hbsp.harvard.edu/product/C0012A-PDF-ENG.

Leath, James. n.d. "Inspiring Athletes through Coaches' Continuous Learning." https://www.jamesleath.com/notes/inspiring-athletes-through-coaches-continuous-learning.

Liebermann, Albert. 2021. *Ganbatte!: The Japanese Art of Always Moving Forward*. Rutland, VT: Tuttle.

McNevin, Mary. 2023. "How to Develop a 5-Year Career Plan." *Harvard Business Review*. September 27, 2023. https://hbr.org/2023/09/how-to-develop-a-5-year-career-plan.

Mendelow, Aubrey. 1991. "Stakeholder Mapping." *Proceedings of the Second International Conference on Information Systems*, pp. 10–24. Cambridge, MA.

Meyer, Nicholas, dir. 2002. *Star Trek II: The Wrath of Khan* [film]. Hollywood, CA: Paramount Pictures.

Meyer, Erin. 2024, July–August. "Build a Corporate Culture that Works," *Harvard Business Review*. https://hbr.org/2024/07/build-a-corporate-culture-that-works.

Miglani, Shveta. 2021. "Examining the Role of Organizational Insiders in Influencing Newcomer Adjustment: An Organizational Ethnographic Study in the Tech Industry." Proquest. https://www.proquest.com/dissertations-theses/examining-role-organizational-insiders/docview/2596462939/se-2.

Nadella, Satya. 2019. *Hit Refresh: The Quest to Rediscover Microsoft's Soul and Imagine a Better Future for Everyone*. New York: Harper Business.

Nooyi, Indira. 2021. *My Life in Full: Work, Family, and Our Future*. New York: Portfolio.

Pomeroy, Robin, and Joe Myers. 2024, January 14. "AI—Artificial Intelligence—at Davos 2024: Here's What to Know." World Economic Forum Meeting. www.weforum.org/stories/2024/01/artificial-intelligence-ai-innovation-technology-davos-2024/.

C., Rajal. 2021, May 6. "Growth Mindset: An Underestimated Game Changer for Leaders." *Forbes Coaches Council Post.* https://www .forbes.com/councils/forbescoachescouncil/2021/05/06/growth-mindset-an-underestimated-game-changer-for-leaders/.

Razzetti, Gustavo. 2021, September 8. "How Amazon Built a Culture of Innovation by Working Backwards." Fearless Culture. https://www .fearlessculture.design/blog-posts/how-amazon-built-a-culture-of-innovation-by-working-backwards.

Rogers, Everett. 1962. *Diffusion of Innovations.* New York: Free Press.

Rometty, Ginni. 2023. *Good Power: Leading Positive Change in Our Lives, Work, and World.* Boston: Harvard Business Review Press.

Sandberg, Sheryl. 2013. *Lean In: Women, Work, and the Will to Lead.* New York: Knopf.

Scholarly Community Encyclopedia. 2022, October 9. "Information Seeking Behavior." https://encyclopedia.pub/entry/28001.

Scott, W. D. (1911). *Increasing Human Efficiency in Business: A Contribution to the Psychology of Business.* New York: Macmillan.

Seidman, Dov. 2011. *How: Why How We Do Anything Means Everything.* Hoboken, NJ: John Wiley & Sons.

Stone, Douglas, and Sheila Heen. 2014. *Thanks for the Feedback: The Science and Art of Receiving Feedback Well (Even When It Is off Base, Unfair, Poorly Delivered, and Frankly, You're Not in the Mood).* New York: Penguin Books.

Taylor, Frederick Winslow. 1911/2012. *Principles of Scientific Management.* Reprint. New York: Dover.

Tristancho, Camilo. 2024, September 26. "Stakeholder Mapping 101: A Quick Guide to Stakeholder Maps." Projectmanager. https://www.project manager.com/blog/stakeholder-mapping-guide.

Veldsman, Dieter, and Ioanna Mantzouridou Onasi. (n.d.) "AI in Learning and Development: Personalizing the Employee Learning Experience." Academy to Innovate HR. Accessed August 10, 2024. https://www.aihr .com/blog/ai-in-learning-and-development/.

Washington Center, The. 2023, June 2. "What Should I Wear? The Ultimate Guide to Workplace Dress Codes." https://resources.twc.edu/articles/what-should-i-wear-to-work.

Wilson, Thomas D. 1981. "On User Studies and Information Needs." *Journal of Documentation*. 37 (1): 3–15. https://doi.org/10.1108/eb026702.

Ware, N. (1924). The industrial worker, 1840-1860: The reaction of American industrial society to the advance of the industrial revolution. Houghton Mifflin.

Zhu, Meng. 2018, September 4. "Why We Procrastinate When We Have Long Deadlines." *Harvard Business Review*. https://hbr.org/2018/08/why-we-procrastinate-when-we-have-long-deadlines.

Acknowledgment

A FEW YEARS BACK, WHILE in London with my family, we immersed ourselves in the city's vibrant energy, from savoring delicious food to indulging in shopping sprees. My son, just eight years old at the time, grew tired during our adventures and simply longed to sit down and read. We stumbled upon a bookstore, where he pleaded for a break to look for a book to read and relax. He looked through all the shelves and found the title he wanted, and a big smile spread across his face. As I took a picture of this tender moment of him engrossed in his reading, blissfully shutting out the bustling world around him, I paused and thought, "Wouldn't it be wonderful to spread this same happiness through a book about my work?" That idea blossomed into a dream, and the dream was nurtured into reality through the support of my family and friends.

This journey began with the boundless curiosity of my son, Kabeer, who has been my wisest critic and greatest support as I navigated the process of writing this book, learning about publishing, and meticulously reviewing every detail. My husband, Mrinal, one of the most hardworking, intelligent, and empathetic leaders I know, has shown me what it truly means to dedicate yourself to your work. Thank you both for your unwavering guidance and support, especially on days when I questioned my goals and needed a reminder of the bigger picture.

Thank you to my parents, who laid a strong foundation in my childhood to ask questions, continuously learn, and always give back. I dedicate my entire work to my mom, Neelam, and my dad, Ramesh. Though you are no longer with me, I feel your blessings guiding me every step of the way. I am grateful for the unwavering support of my sister, Shaila, my brother-in-law, Manu, and my nephew, Rohan.

Achieving your dreams truly takes a village. I am incredibly grateful for my family, who always believed in my work and pushed me to do my best: Kirty, Arun, Gunjan, and Mehul. My colleagues and friends, Sameena and Xiaofang, who reviewed my work, provided invaluable advice, and shared their insights, helping me learn and grow. My group of peer authors and friends—Teresa Sande, Cynthia Owyoung, Larry McAlister, Regina Lawless, Melissa Daimler, Brandon Carson, and Jo Miller—have been instrumental in this journey.

Special thanks to my wonderful editor, Deborah Ager, whose patience with my rewrites and positive energy kept me motivated to reach the finish line. My designer, Becky Bayne, skillfully transformed my vision and inspirations into the beautiful design of my book. My marketing friends, Bhawna Sharma Puri and Pooja Ahuja, provided essential support in bringing this project to life. The same gratitude goes to my team at Wiley, Brian Neill and Gabriela Mancuso.

I extend my heartfelt thanks to my teachers, mentors, peers, and colleagues from the past two decades, including David Blake Willis, Jack Keenan, Manjula Talreja, Siva Sivaram, Drew Henry, Thy Tran, and Cher Whee Sim. Their support and advice have been invaluable.

A heartfelt appreciation for my professional network and leaders who shaped this book with their insights and experiences: Anneka Gupta, Anjali Sharma, Brandon Clark, Brandon Sammut, Brandon Carson, Nithya Ruff, Marrisa Morisson, Josh Bersin, Bill Pelster, and Rob Beard,

It would be remiss of me not to acknowledge the organizations I have worked with and served at: Google, Salesforce, SanDisk, Palo Alto Networks, LiveRamp, Micron, and CityYear. These experiences and the people I met in each organization have significantly contributed to my learning and growth.

काल करे सो आज कर, आज करे सो अब पल में पूरलय होएगी, बहुरि करोगे कब

Do the work that needs to be done now.
There is no other time than now.

—Kabir, Poet and Saint

About the Author

DR. SHVETA MIGLANI is a visionary leader in learning and development, organizational growth, and career transformation. With over two decades of experience, she has shaped the futures of professionals and organizations across the globe, holding strategic roles at tech giants such as Micron Technology, GlobalFoundries, SanDisk, Palo Alto Networks, Google, and Salesforce. A passionate advocate for talent empowerment, Dr. Miglani has trained over 5,000 professionals across 10 countries, helping individuals unlock their potential and organizations thrive. She is also the recipient of the California Diversity Award.

A sought-after speaker, Dr. Miglani has shared her expertise and taught at leadership panels including engagements with Josh Bersin, USC Marshall School of Business, George Mason University, and HR Learning forums.

She crafted this book to equip professionals with the insights and strategies needed to navigate pivotal career transitions with confidence and success. Having mentored thousands of leaders and rising talents across the globe, she recognized a common challenge: Many professionals step into new roles or promotions without a clear roadmap, leading to uncertainty and missed opportunities. Driven by a passion for leadership excellence and talent development, this strategic guide helps individuals confidently take on new responsibilities, accelerate their success, and thrive in their evolving careers.

Rooted in research from her PhD work, this book also features insights from interviews with leaders at Amazon, Zapier, ZipRecruiter, and Adobe, offering readers firsthand wisdom from executives who have successfully navigated career transitions. These voices, combined with Dr. Miglani's own expertise, provide practical strategies to master new leadership expectations, build credibility, and make an impact from day 1. With this guide, Dr. Miglani aims to equip professionals with the confidence and clarity they need to excel in their new roles and shape a successful career trajectory.

You may contact Dr. Miglani at www.shvetamiglani.com or via LinkedIn at: www.linkedin.com/in/shvetamiglani/.

Index

211

Index

213

Index